Other Books by Alexander Humez and Nicholas Humez

ABC Et Cetera
Alpha to Omega
Latin for People

ZERO TO LAZY EIGHT

The Romance of Numbers

Alexander Humez,

Nicholas Humez, and

Joseph Maguire

A Touchstone Book
Published by Simon & Schuster
New York   London   Toronto   Sydney   Tokyo   Singapore

TOUCHSTONE
Rockefeller Center
1230 Avenue of the Americas
New York, New York 10020

First Touchstone Edition 1994
TOUCHSTONE and colophon are registered trademarks
of Simon & Schuster, Inc.

Designed by Irving Perkins Associates
Manufactured in the United States of America

10 9 8 7 6 5 4 3 2

Library of Congress Cataloging-in-Publication Data

Humez, Alexander.
    Zero to lazy eight : the romance of numbers / Alexander Humez,
Nicholas Humez, and Joseph Maguire.
          p.   cm.
    Includes index.
    1. Numerals—Quotations, maxims, etc. 2. Numerals—Social
aspects. 3. Mathematics. I. Humez, Nicholas D. II. Maguire,
Joseph. III. Title.
QA141.H86   1993
513.2—dc20   93–13204
                                                                    CIP

ISBN: 0-671-74282-5
        0-671-74281-7 (Pbk.)

To David Ernest Humez, 1917–1993

CONTENTS

ACKNOWLEDGMENTS

We would like to express our gratitude to the following people for their indispensable help in bringing this book to life and fostering its well-being: Andy Adler, Thomas Battle, André Bernard, Gail Bradney, Joe Chapman, Mark Colan, Paul DeVore, Jo Diggs, the late Sterling Dow, Greg Doyle, Malcah Yaeger Dror, Lee Edwards, Ross A. Faneuf, Peggy Ferrari, the late Robert Franz, Douglas French, Harold W. Gleason Jr., Josh Goldman, J. Arthur Greenwood, Gail Gutradt, Ross Hagstoz, Dori Hale, Jerold Harmatz, Bertha Hatvary, Frank Holan, Ilse Holan, Jennifer Holan, Andrea Humez, the late David E. Humez, Elisabeth G. Humez, Jean Humez, Sally Jans-Thorpe, Phil Jensen, Edward Kearney, Katy Kline, Denise Lee, Marina Leslie, Philip Metcalf, Elizabeth Michaud, a monk of Mount Royal, Paul Monsky, Mike Newman, Linda Sampey, Heidi von Schreiner, Jon Strand, Alan Taylor, Pat Washburn, and Nancy Wilson.

PREFACE

THIS BOOK IS about numbers—specifically, the Arabic ones we all know and love—and the ways in which we think about numbers or take them for granted in colloquial expressions: *at sixes and sevens, dressed to the nines, a baker's dozen,* and so on. Just as language shapes thought, so numbers influence language; it would be impossible to imagine a society that could read and write and yet had no numerical skills whatsoever—couldn't count, couldn't tell time, couldn't transact any business aside from barter, and even then couldn't tell when a trade came out even. Indeed, the very use of *even* to denote both a class of numbers and a relationship between quantities suggests how deeply ingrained numbers are in our daily thoughts and actions.

Literacy is often used as a gauge of a society's standard of living and degree of sophistication. Recently it has been joined by "numeracy"—the ability to manipulate numbers. Articles have been written in the scientific press asking whether our numeracy has kept pace with our technology. Opinions vary; clearly most of us can do simple arithmetic with paper and pencil—though the ready availability of the pocket calculator has many of us somewhat out of practice at this. Some have said that we are indeed less "numerate" than we were a couple of generations ago, citing an apparent decline in our ability to eyeball a pile of something and guess how many are in it. But nobody questions that numeracy in some form is here to stay, and that we are on the whole better at figures than, say, the Romans.

We have the Arabic numerals to thank for this, for the Roman system was cumbersome indeed, not much more than a system of tally marks, albeit a very fancy one. It was an extremely clumsy system even for simple tasks like addition and subtraction, and multiplication and division were worse. It was also pitifully inadequate for handling very large numbers—and it had no zero.

The beauty of Arabic numerals lies in great part in their economy. Ten symbols suffice to represent any number of any size. The Roman numeral for the Arabic 3,087, for example, would be MMMLXXXVII, which takes twice as much pencil just to write, never mind computing with it. The righthand-most numeral of 3,087 is 7, which represents seven (i.e., itself); but the numbers to the left of it represent tens (eight of them), hundreds (in this case, none), and thousands (three of them). Indeed, much, much bigger numbers can be written without trouble in the same way. This was a truly revolutionary generative feature, one that left the Romans in the dust. The other revolutionary feature is zero, equal to nothing (or nothingness) and doubling as a placeholder (as in the hundreds column of 3,087), a concept utterly foreign to Romans or to Greeks before them.

It is the elegance of such a system that commends itself to the user, just as any good tool bears the implicit slogan, "Once you have used me, you'll never use any other." With the exceptions of analog clock and watch faces, and inscriptions on neoclassical public buildings putting on airs, Roman numerals are now virtually extinct. The adoption of Arabic numerals resembled the acquisition of a new grammar—and a new world view—which describes events well in the numerical real world and has, in addition, tremendous powers, in this case the ability to create new numbers out of whole cloth and to have them behave predictably. It has been said that any scientific revolution behaves like the Gestalt switch of looking at an Escher drawing of ducks that, when you look again, seems to have turned into a picture of rabbits (or vice versa). For the Westerner acquiring Arabic numerals, the world was never the same again.

Mathematics is a thing of the mind, at least by comparison with the inductive reasoning that tells you to watch your step in the woods or to remember your bug repellent. Even though most of our real-world life is lived empirically, none of us is a strictly inductive thinker, for every time we perform the humblest of numerical calculations, we are assuming certain axioms and deducing from them. We may memorize, as children, that $2 + 2 = 4$; that is a definition. But we do not memorize the fact that $22 + 22 = 44$. At the very least, we are taking a definition and applying a generative rule to it, with predictable results.

This is also what we do when we make up a "new" sentence, either in our native language or in a language with which we are unfamiliar. In the latter case, it is much easier to catch oneself in the act: We may never have "heard" the sentence before but we can build it using spare parts of speech and a few grammatical rules. This is not to say that one doesn't occasionally make up sentences that don't work, any more than one always gets one's sums right—one's grammar may get a little rusty from disuse—but in both cases we know that there is a "right" answer, and either assume we are succeeding until someone tells us otherwise, or else recognize our goof and try, try again.

And just as language, by allowing the expression of certain ideas, colors our view of the world by the things it allows (and doesn't allow) us to say about it, so our numerical sense lets us interpret the quantities of the world, to make statements about what was, and predictions about what will or might conceivably be, limited only by our imagination and familiarity with the axioms and rules of the mathematical game. To the extent that numbers say anything about the real world, they do so unfailingly and incorruptibly—at least until the next scientific revolution comes to alter our perception of the universe as we know it.

We've come to appreciate that words change over time, and change their meanings too; syntax and grammar change as well, if more slowly. Every language alive today has impermanence as a corollary of its very vitality. What's more surprising and less understood: Numbers and our numerical system also evolve. Mathematical advances are like any other: Growth in our understanding coincides with growth in our language, be that language one of words or one of numbers. Throughout this book you will find many examples of the expansion of the notion of number over the course of history. Such expansions are not limited to the outer reaches of abstract mathematics; a mere four centuries ago, most folks wouldn't think to write ¼ as .25, and would have no idea how to calculate with it that way. The world of numbers is subject to the same kind of growth as the world of words, and the effects of these changes reach to the humblest shop clerk. Nevertheless, a substantial portion of our counting system has remained constant for some time now: Four stones on Pericles's Acropolis are still the same four stones today (unless they get moved or split by frost or their fourness is otherwise compromised by external circumstance); and $2 + 2$ equals 4 just as much today as ever it did in Scythia or Sumer.

Perhaps it is this perceived durability of numbers that has given them such a permanent place in our conscious and subconscious minds. Numbers shape language, and vice versa. They pop up even in our most casual utterances. The awesome power numeracy has for describing, predicting, and manipulating the real world might easily lead one to ascribe magical power to numbers—as people have done, in all times and places including ours. How many thirteenth floors simply don't exist in many a twentieth-century building? We are naturally encouraged to be rational about numbers when, as children, we are first taught to cipher (a word that means, significantly, both 'zero' and 'code'); yet even people perfectly well aware of the immensity of the odds will play their "lucky number" in the lottery week after week without a qualm, or, for that matter, a win. That lottery sales are a booming business says less about the rationality of the human race than it does about the pervasiveness of numbers in our psyche, making themselves at home even where deductive reason fears to tread.

This book, then, will talk about some numbers and the expressions we use to employ them. Each chapter centers on an integer from zero to thirteen, with a final chapter, appropriately enough, about the infinite (conventionally represented by something very much like an eight lying on its side, which in cowhands' branding terminology is called a *lazy eight*). This is not a mathematics textbook (you may breathe a sigh of relief here, in case you were worried), although we shall have some things to say about selected mathematical topics, particularly number theory, but also graph theory, set theory, and probability. Nor is it—despite some stories we shall tell—a history of mathematical or scientific thought, a topic worth books and books by itself. Instead, this is a book about people and the part numbers play in how they look at and talk about their universe. If, as C. P. Snow has said, there are "two cultures"—humanists and scientists, who don't always understand each other—we hope that this book will narrow the gap a little bit, or at least demystify both sides, and show what sort of worldview follows when language adapts numbers to its own ends.

ZERO

ZERO IS WHERE it all begins, the clean slate. We speak of *zero-sum games* (in which anyone who wins anything does so only at the equal expense of the losers), *zero hour* (the time at which a military operation begins), *ground zero* (the impact point of a bomb, particularly a nuclear one), to *zero in on* something (getting it precisely in the cross hairs), *zero degrees* of temperature—which, depending on the scale you use, can be the freezing point of water (Centigrade), fortified wine (Fahrenheit), or the universe (Kelvin); the last, a bit chillier than $-273°$ C or $-459°$ F, is aptly called *absolute zero*.

Zero is the only number that is neither positive nor negative. As such, it represents a quantity: If *three* is the name we give to the number of items in a trilogy, a trinity, or a triad, *zero* is our name for the number of items in an empty, or null set, i.e., one having no members. This is not the same as saying the set doesn't exist; in fact, we can and do make valid assertions about null sets, as Nancy Friday did when discussing the fact that none of the women whom she interviewed for her book on women's erotic fantasies, *My Secret Garden*, reported experiencing fantasies of prostitution.

The confusion between "nothing(ness)" and "an empty set (a level playing field, point of origin, etc.)" was one reason it took so long for there to be a symbol for zero in the first place. After all, if all you're doing is counting sheep, and there aren't any, your job is done before it starts. For much of history, a crying need to represent the quantity of zero was not at all obvious, and zero was conspicuously absent from most early number systems. So zero is not, historically speaking, where it all begins if by *it* we mean numeration. For that matter, zero is not the same as a clean slate: The math student who leaves one question blank, then argues that he should get full credit when the answer turns out to be zero, won't get very far (except perhaps in politics).

The Romans could represent any quantity up to the largest needed in everyday life, except for zero. Representing a number in Roman numerals was like adding weights to a pan—a thousand weight, a five-hundred weight, two one-hundred weights, a fifty weight, two ten weights, a five, and a single would be represented by the Romans as MDCCLXXVI and by us as 1,776. Unlike the signs used for numeration in Greek, Hebrew, and other languages (in which consecutive letters of the alphabet were assigned consecutively higher numbers), the Roman numerals (I, V, X, L , C, D, M) look to have been merely influenced by the local alphabet; the represented quantities show tidy divisions of fives and tens, a tipoff that the Romans let their fingers have a hand in their number system.

Even without a character for zero, Latin could accommodate numbers like 1,006: MVI. In contrast, the Babylonians used a kind of zero as a placeholder, much the way we do today. We write and interpret 306 as 3 hundreds (tens of tens) plus 0 tens plus 6 ones—that is:

$$(3 \times 10 \times 10) + (0 \times 10) + (6 \times 1)$$

Babylonians, using 60 as their counting base, would interpret 306 like this:

$$(3 \times 60 \times 60) + (0 \times 60) + (6 \times 1)$$

The Babylonians could write numbers that looked like 2,205, but not ones like 2,200, zero as a final placeholder being an afterthought. Still, one can't have everything, and Babylon had improved significantly upon Sumer, which had had three separate accounting systems to keep track of land, livestock, and grain—each with its own symbols!

The superiority of the Babylonians' number system helped them accomplish much in the field of astronomy, but the Romans, toddling along with neither a zero numeral nor the concept of positional notation (that which lets 3 represent 300, or 3,000, or 3/10, depending on its position), managed to erect the Colosseum and the Appian Way, both of which have survived 2,000 years (and counting).

Across the Aegean, Archimedes's treatise *The Sand Reckoner* showed Greek readers of the second century B.C. how some minor modifications to the Greek alphabetic numeration system would allow it to handle numbers of the greatest magnitude then imaginable (e.g., the number of grains of sand on a beach, whence came Archimedes's title). Roman mathematicians were undoubtedly acquainted with this work but do not seem to have knocked themselves out to make their own system any more parsimonious as a result, because this would require abandoning the weights-in-a-pan metaphor so fundamental to Roman numeration. For the most part, in antiquity (indeed, up to the industrial revolution), the quantities that people needed to calculate were not all that large.

It wasn't until 1202 that the mathematician Leonardo of Pisa, better known as Fibonacci (i.e., 'son of Bonacci'), found it necessary to write his most famous treatise, the *Liber Abaci* (The Abacus Book). This was essentially a polemic advocating the adoption of the decimal Arabic (or, as Fibonacci more accurately termed them, Indian) numbers (including zero) in place of the cumbersome Roman numerals.

There is actually very little about the abacus in the *Liber Abaci:* Fibonacci just mentions it in the second paragraph, where he tells how he came to write the treatise in the first place. His father, a customs official stationed in the African market center of Burgia, urged Fibonacci to learn how to use the abacus from a local mathematician, who also introduced him to a lot of other interesting ideas, including Arabic numbers.

The word *abacus* arrived in Latin as part of a boxed set, an acquisition from the Greeks, who also supplied the notion of calculating with movable counters. There is some disagreement on whether the source of Greek *abax* is Phoenician *abak* 'sand' or

Hebrew *abhaq* 'dust,' but the idea was the same: You strewed sand or dust on a board or surface on which you could then write or move counters around.

When a culture borrows an idea from a neighboring society, the word and idea arrive simultaneously, and when we use a borrowed term we are, at least to a certain extent, thinking about something in the same way the people did from whom we appropriated the word and the idea. Both the words and our notions of philosophy owe much to the Greeks, just as the Romans gave us the benefit of their extensive practical knowledge in civil engineering and jurisprudence, generously throwing in the terminology for free. So it went with *abacus*.

The earliest abacus with counters seems to have been a board with grooves in it, and a number of ancient sources suggest that it originated with the Babylonians—a credible idea, given their invention of positional notation. But it is also possible that it originated in India, coming to the West in the hands of arithmetically savvy traders. That it would have spread easily across borders is hardly surprising: As a computational tool, the abacus works quickly and accurately. Its single drawback is that it has no way of representing zero; consequently, it's impossible to tell an unused abacus from one whose owner has just solved an arithmetic problem yielding the answer 0—at least not without a thermometer to measure for residual heat of friction.

Most of the abaci one sees nowadays are oriental ones, since Asian shopkeepers continue to use their version of the device to this day. The Chinese name for it is *suan pan*, and the first known examples of it date from the twelfth century A.D. The counters of the suan pan are beads strung on wires. The Romans came close to this: France's Bibliothèque Nationale preserves a brass abacus in which the counting board's grooves for pebbles have become a series of slots with movable *claviculi* ('little nails'). This abacus is good for reckoning numbers from 1 to 1,000,000—and has a slot for quarter fractions as well.

The Latin for 'pebble' is *calculus,* the name applied to the branch of mathematics invented independently by Sir Isaac Newton and

Gottfried Wilhelm Leibniz in the latter half of the seventeenth century. It is also, via the Latin verb *calculāre* (literally, 'to pebble,' figuratively, 'to do arithmetic'), the reason we call those little machines pocket *calculators*.

The Greek verb *psēphizein* meant the same thing as *calculāre: psēphos* was Greek for 'pebble.' *Psēphos* is probably related to *psein* 'to wear smooth, rub,' which gives the *-psest* of English *palimpsest* 'recycled parchment' (literally, 'scraped again'). *Psēphizomai* is the first-person mediopassive or "middle" voice, literally meaning something like 'I pebble,' and this is what Athenians said when they placed a pebble in an urn to cast their ballots at the Athenian law courts. (Sometimes the *psēphoi* for acquittal and condemnation were distinguished by the former being called *plērēis* 'whole,' and the latter, *tetrypemenai* 'bored,' the former being ordinary round pebbles while the latter had holes bored through them. Since jurors presumably did the boring themselves, this system incorporated a wholesome presumption of innocence requiring a positive effort to convict.)

In addition to pebbles for the courts, Athenians used broken shards of pottery (*ostraka*) on which they wrote the names of those they voted to ostracize. Athenians also used lots (*kyamoi*) for the election of officials—*ballot* is unrelated to *lot,* being, rather, from Italian *ballota* ('little ball').

In English, we *cast* a ballot. The word is Scandinavian in origin—it does not appear in other Germanic languages, which have variants of *warp* for what you do at election time instead—but its meanings in English are legion, amounting to over sixty column-inches in the *Century Dictionary*. In addition to all the meanings of *cast* clearly related to its meaning of 'throw,' a printer speaks of *casting off copy,* i.e., figuring out how many column-inches a piece will run when typeset; theatrical directors *cast parts* (and those who are chosen for them together make up the *cast*); sailors *cast a vessel,* bringing it about to have the wind on one side; founders *cast* molten metal into a mold; we speak of someone having an unhealthy *cast,* i.e., a sickly complexion; and the *first cast* in brewing is the amount of water added to the original mash in the vat. Up through the Enlightenment, *cast* was a synonym for 'vomit,' while to the modern-day C programmer, *cast* is what you do to a variable to change its data type. (*Caste*, on the other hand, is unrelated; this term for the four classes of Hindu society is from a Portuguese cognate of *chaste*.)

Many English expressions with *cast* are straight translations of French ones with *jeter:* Something that's cast is a *jeton*, which also means 'token,' and was the word employed for the pebbles used on the French version of the counting board that had grooves in it. Such a board was called a *comptoir*, whence came English *counter* 'thing used for counting' (from the root that underlies Latin *computāre* 'to calculate, reckon, compute,' itself a compound form of *putāre* 'to ponder, assess, think') and 'flat surface on which business is transacted, food is prepared or served,' and so on.

Token is not, as one might guess, from *take*, but from an Indo-European root (**deik̂-*) which means something like 'teach' or 'show.' The same root underlies the *dig-* of Latin *digitus* 'finger' (originally, 'index finger,' because you point with it), the *-dex* of *index*, and the *-dic-* of *indicate, indict, predict*, and the other compounds built on Latin *dīcere* 'to say.' It is from the use of fingers for counting and measuring that *digitus* came to mean '(Arabic) number.'

The words *number* and *numeral* come from Latin *numerus*, whence came French *nombre* and *numéro*, which are used, respectively, to indicate quantity and position in a series (*un nombre entier* is 'a whole number, i.e., an integer' while *numéro quatre-vingt six* means 'number 86'—which, in America at least, is also lunch-counter slang for 'we don't have any left'). Speakers of French use the term *chiffre* to refer to a numeral, i.e., the orthographic figure that represents a number: *Chiffres romains* are 'Roman numerals.'

Figure comes via Latin and French from an Indo-European root (**deiĝh-*) meaning 'knead,' as in clay or dough. So, in fact, do *dough*, the *-dise* of *paradise*, and the *-dy* of *lady* (whose original literal meaning was 'loaf kneader'). The same root underlies the Latin verb *fingere* 'to mold,' which has a horde of derivatives of its own, including the English words *effigy, fiction, fictitious, figment*, and, of course, *figure* itself, with all its compounds. *Figure* seems to have first been used to refer to numbers as signs ('' '8' is the figure for what the Romans meant when they wrote 'VIII' ''), much as the French use *chiffre* today. Later, by analogy, the term came to apply to the manipulation of those figures, and still later, to any kind of thought (as in ''Go figure!'').

French *chiffre* and English *zero* and *cipher* all come from Arabic *sifr,* which was the name for zero and literally meant 'empty.' Like *figure, cipher* also became a verb that (like *chiffrer* in French) still means 'calculate, do arithmetic' among some older people in the rural United States. But *cipher* originally meant just plain 'zero,' whence the following alphanumeric puzzle, printed by R. R. Ripley (of ''Believe It or Not!'' fame) two generations ago:

> U 0 a 0, but I 0 thee
> O 0 no 0, but O 0 me.
> O let not my 0 a mere 0 go,
> But 0 my 0 I 0 thee so.

This is to be decoded as:

> You sigh for a cipher, but I sigh for thee.
> O sigh for no cipher, but O sigh for me.
> O let not my sigh for a mere cipher go,
> But sigh for my sigh, for I sigh for thee so.

Which brings us to the other meaning of *cipher:* 'code.' One speaks, for example, of *substitution ciphers,* where one letter of the alphabet is systematically used for another. The cipher used by the emperor Augustus substituted the next letter in the alphabet for the one he meant, so that *hasta* ('spear') became *ibtub.* (But *fornix*— 'vaulted arch'—would read *gpsokaa,* because Augustus used *aa* to stand for *x,* the last letter of the Roman alphabet until it borrowed *y* and *z* from Greek.) *Encryption*—literally, 'the act of hiding something' (from Greek *krypton* 'hidden thing,' whence came the name of the noble gas *krypton,* as well as English *crypt*)—has taken on the specialized meaning of 'the act of coding.' Ciphers are not the only means of encryption: Another kind works with two matching templates. The writer inscribes the intended words on a first template and then surrounds them on the page with a much larger, seemingly innocuous cover letter. The recipient puts the second template over the blather and correctly reads the original message. Like an acrostic, this kind of code works by applying a specific, preagreed-upon rule or set of rules to filter the "real" message out from its packaging.

The disadvantage of templates is that one must spend a great deal of time thinking up ingenious letters about how the valiant troops are the main**stay** of the war effort and a constant source of inspiration to the folks at **home,** especially during these un**for**tuna**te, t**roublesome times (to warn of the upcoming military action planned by the Viet Cong for the month of Tet)—otherwise, the fact that something clandestine is going on becomes a little obvious to the onlooker. It is a lot easier to send and receive messages in what looks like gobble-dygook to the outside observer—that way, to be sure, everybody knows you're transmitting in code, but nobody (you hope) can tell what it means. During World War II, the Allies cracked the German cipher before the bombing of Coventry, so they knew the raid was coming. The agonizing decision not to warn the inhabitants cost many lives in that city when the Luftwaffe came, but undoubtedly hastened the end of the war because it allowed the Nazis' signals to go on being intercepted and exploited without their knowledge, whereas an evacuation of Coventry would have warned Germany that the code had been broken.

Sometimes the best code is simply talking in a language nobody else knows, as when Navajo radiomen handled sensitive communications for the American army in the Pacific theater. Or one can make up one's own: George Washington's cipher was a book in which each word or phrase was represented by a three-digit number. Such strings of figures, each arbitrarily assigned in a codebook held by only the sender and receiver, can be surprisingly decryption-resistant too.

Not all codes are for hiding things. Take the vanishing genre of alphanumeric telephone mnemomics, words that also spell something on the telephone dial or keypad (e.g., dialing NERVOUS in Boston gets you the current time and temperature). Forty years ago, picking up the phone connected the user directly with an operator. There was no dial at all; one spoke the name of the exchange, then five digits of the number itself: "Lexington 9-1212," say. When rotary phones came into vogue (in the greater Boston area, this was in the mid-fifties), phone numbers became seven digits; some retained the numerical equivalent of what had been the first two letters of the town's exchange; others got something like it. (For Arlington, Massachusetts, the new exchange was *ALgonquin,* which was close to *A'Lington,* the way the name of the town is actually pronounced by most of its inhabitants.)

The ASCII (American Standard Code for Information Interchange) code expresses characters of the computer "alphabet" in terms of numbers between 0 and 127 (or 255 in extended ASCII). This alphabet includes uppercase letters (A through Z), lowercase letters (a through z), numerals (0 through 9), assorted punctuation marks, and some nonprinting characters used for internal computer controls. ASCII numbers 048 to 057 designate the Arabic numerals 0 to 9; 065 to 090 are the capital letters A to Z; and so on.

The ASCII code distinguishes among the character for zero (048), the blank space (032), and the null character (000). Within an electronic message, 048 means that the message includes the character 0, while 032 means that the message includes a blank space, and 000— the null character—probably means you've reached the end of the message, akin to saying "Over" to signify the end of a radio transmission, though it may just as well signify that something got lost in transmission and all bets are off.

Among the better known numerical codes in the United States is the ZIP code, *zip* ostensibly standing for Zone Improvement Program, although alacrity was surely on the mind of the Postmaster General as well when the U.S. Postal Service first replaced two-digit postal zones with five-digit codes. *Zip* is, ironically, among the many folk expressions for *zero,* particularly common in the scoring of games: *Goose egg* is used by American bowlers to refer to a turn (called a *frame,* presumably from the boxes on the scoring sheet) without a pin down, while *love* for 'zero' in tennis comes from French *l'oeuf* 'the egg.'

Zilch—already common enough by the end of World War II that the founding editor of *The New Yorker,* Harold Ross, explicitly discouraged writers and editors from running stories where the nebbishy protagonist was named *Joe Zilch*—is, like *zip,* alliterative for 'zero.' *Zip* also carries connotations of closure or finality by analogy with *zipper,* originally an early twentieth-century trademark for a metal slide fastener—itself coined from the much earlier *zip* 'animation,' which had been around for a century.

A *zero* is an ineffectual person—what a computer designer would call a *null op,* as in "That guy's a zero, a real null op." *Null op* is short for *null operation,* an internal computer operation that performs no calculation or data manipulation whatever. Your personal computer cycles through millions of null operations while you, deciding how to begin the next sentence, stare at the screen.

Zero as a personal insult is grounded in the arithmetic properties of zero: it has no effect on any addend—i.e., on any quantity that is to be added to some other quantity—$(n + 0 = n)$, no effect on a minuend—i.e., on any quantity from which something is to be subtracted—$(n - 0 = n)$, and a nullifying effect on any multiplicand—i.e., on any quantity that is to be multiplied by another—$(n \times 0 = 0)$.

Division, anyone? Well, when you multiply n times m and neither multiplicand (n nor m) is zero, the equation reveals two possible inverse divisions. Let's say that $n = 3$ and $m = 4$. Because $3 \times 4 = 12$, we have these two divisions:

$$\frac{12}{3} = 4 \qquad \frac{12}{4} = 3$$

In each equation, the product of the right side and the divisor (the bottom of the fraction) equals the dividend (the top of the fraction). But if one of the multiplicands is zero, we can find only one meaningful division. Because $3 \times 0 = 0$, we get:

$$\frac{0}{3} = 0 \qquad \frac{0}{0} \stackrel{?}{=} 3$$

The left equation makes sense, $0 \times 3 = 0$. But the right equation tries to assert that $0/0 = 3$ because $3 \times 0 = 0$. But we could build a similar equation, asserting that $0/0 = 4$ because $4 \times 0 = 0$. The division $0/0$ cannot equal both 3 and 4, so the expression $0/0$ must remain undefined.

Even when the dividend is not zero, a zero divisor is not allowed. The equation

$$\frac{3}{0} = ?$$

could never make sense, no matter how we replace the "?." *Nothing* times 0 equals 3, so the division 3/0 has no answer.

This way lies wailing and gnashing of teeth, and the best answer is simply to avoid getting into equations where you're caught with zeros in compromising positions. After all, there are plenty of numbers to play with.

ONE

In the beginning, all things were one. A single point of immense energy burst forth into everything in the universe in a primordial explosion astronomers have dubbed *the Big Bang*. Within its first few seconds of existence, the rapidly expanding cosmos was filled with high-energy plasma, coalescing into a flurry of subatomic particles called *quarks* (also known as *aces*), which in turn formed the protons, electrons, and other exotic particles that make up matter as we know it. A nameless scientific wag summarized the history of the universe to date as follows:

> First there was nothing.
> Then there was something.
> Then there was hydrogen.
> Then there was dirty hydrogen.

Lao-tzu, founder of Taoism, put it somewhat differently: ''The sky attained Oneness and became clear; the earth attained Oneness and became calm.'' Elsewhere in the *Tao-te Ching* he writes:

> Tao gave birth to One,
> One gave birth to Two,
> Two gave birth to Three,
> Three gave birth to all the myriad things.

The idea of cosmic Oneness intrigued Greek pre-Socratic thinkers. Xenophanes of Colophon, who flourished in the middle of the sixth century B.C., asserted that God is one. This was by no means a novel idea in the eastern Mediterranean—the inhabitants of Palestine had worshipped a single god for centuries, ever since the Jews arrived and kicked the polytheistic Canaanites out; and the heretic king Akhenaton of Egypt briefly experimented with monotheism, though Egypt rejected it after he was succeeded by the boy-king Tutankhamen—but the idea created something of a stir in the Greek philosophical community.

According to Plutarch (writing in the first century A.D.), the Stoics opted for a compromise, believing "that among the gods, of whom there are a very great number, there is only one who is eternal and immortal; all the rest they [the Stoics] believe to have come into existence and to be liable to extinction." Led by Parmenides of Elea, who may have studied with Xenophanes while the latter was purportedly vacationing in Italy during the unpleasantness with the Persians in Colophon, the Eleatics put their own spin on the idea of Oneness: All that is real (Being) forms a single whole.

In the Greco-Roman world at large, monotheism flew in the face of the official religion and its Olympian pantheon. One of the charges made against Socrates was that he denied the existence of the gods. The Romans' chief problem with Christians was the latter's stubborn refusal to acknowledge the divinities from whom the Roman state derived its authority, whether Jupiter Greatest and Best or the deified emperor Augustus. Such a denial was tantamount to insurrection; Roman society tolerated many different religions and just couldn't fathom one that wouldn't tolerate theirs.

It has been said that the difference between Christians and Jews is that the latter are monotheistic, while the former believe in one God who is three Persons—and that both are distinguished from the Muslims, who believe that there is only one True God. Maybe so. Certainly privileging one's own version of the Supreme Being to the exclusion of all others has allowed for an awful lot of head bashing in the name of orthodoxy among the adherents of these faiths over the centuries. It is interesting that it was not until 1860 that the eminent Sanskritist and scholar of religions, Max Müller, coined the term *henotheism* to denote 'a belief in one god [as opposed to One God],' in other words, a nonproprietary monotheism.

Henotheism is not so named because it is a belief that either a chicken or Henny Youngman is divine, but because *heno-* is a combinatorial form of Greek *heis, hen* 'one.' *Heno-* looks as though it ought to be cognate with Latin *unus* 'one,' the Latin derivatives *uncial, inch, ounce,* the Germanic *e-* of *eleven,* and, of course, *one* itself, all of which derive from an Indo-European root (**oino-*) meaning 'single, sole.' But appearances can be deceiving: Greek *heis, hen* actually derives from a different Indo-European root (**sem-*), the one that underlies the *sin-* of *single;* the *sim-* of *simple;* the *sem-* of *assembly* (a grouping of people into a single "body"); the *sem-* of Latin *semper* 'always' or 'once and for all'; the *homo-* of *homosexual* (and the *he-* of *heterosexual*); the *San-* of *Sanskrit;* the *So-* of *Soviet;* the English words *same* and *seem;* perhaps the (Latinate) *semi-* and the (Hellenic) *hemi-,* both of *hemisemidemiquaver* (British English for 'sixty-fourth note,' literally, 'half-half-half-eighth note'); and the *san(d)-* of *sandblind* (an archaic English word meaning 'half/partially blind').

Throughout history, the first person singular has been the most stable member of the Indo-European pronoun family (the second person singular running a close second), at least as far as preserving the original items of vocabulary with which we talk about ourselves. Means of expressing third-personhood, on the other hand, have always been the most varied across the Indo-European family. Perhaps one can get away with saying anything about someone who's not there to contradict it, as suggested by the Haitian Creole distinction between *nou* 'we, us, you all' and *yo* 'they, them.'

The number *one* figures in a host of folk expressions. We speak of being *at one (with oneself),* of *looking out for number one* (i.e., *oneself*), of being *number one,* current since the days of the Korean War as slang for 'tops,' and still thriving in urban territorial-assertive graffiti: *Crips/Bloods/Ostrogoths #1.* Vietnam-era slang carried this idea further: 1 = great, 10 = lousy, and 1,000 was so bad as to be off the scale. In the Newspeak of George Orwell's *1984,* perhaps the equivalent was *doubleplusungood.* The best pilots in World War I were called *aces,* owing to this one-spot card's ranking above the face cards in poker. In the euphemistic universe of schoolroom potty discourse, *number one* refers to micturation, *number two* to defecation, #1 being considered a more urgent call of nature than #2.

Entertainers speak of the *one-night stand*—the music stand is synecdoche for the entire gig—and the *one-liner* (the joke that is its own punchline). The all-American *one-horse town* has survived the advent of the electric trolley and the commuter train as a metaphor for the little village that time has passed by. Such a hamlet is sometimes also called a *one-eye(d) town,* from a popular belief that the eyes grow closer together in succeeding generations of rural inbreeding.

English has a number of expressions—like *one-eyed*—betokening mental or social deficiency (e.g., *to row with one oar, to play with less than a full deck, to be a brick short of a full load, to be a day late and a dollar short*) that suggest completeness, less a little something. However, there is a flip side too: *One* can also be used as a generic increment over a nice round number: Disney's *101 Dalmatians,* Scheherazade's *Thousand and One* (a.k.a. *Arabian*) *Nights,* and Tuli Kupferberg's *1001 Ways to Beat the Draft* being but three of the many literary classics that exemplify this notion. We speak of *one too many* (usually in reference to drinks) and of *going someone one better. One-upmanship* was coined in 1955 by the British satirosociologist Stephen Potter, another instance of putting a name to a recognized concept that had been waiting for one.

So why should *numbers* have names? Some cultures have lacked words for quantities greater than two or three, even though members of these cultures could distinguish among higher numbers in recognizing where these nameless higher numbers occur within a sequence. One way was by matching the things being counted with some other ordered set, one to one, such as parts of the body (including but not limited to fingers). The shepherd who yesterday enumerated his flock by pointing in order to his ten fingers, his two feet, his two knees, and his left elbow, today knows he's missing part of his flock if, following the same sequence, he only gets to one knee.

But beyond mere count-and-match, many calculations (such as figuring out how many chickens you can get if you swap three sheep for them at the going rate) require that the language have a sequence of names for quantities like *one, two, three,* and so on—an infinite thoroughfare of numbers any one of which could legitimately arise during discourse, thereby obliging the speaker to refer to the number by name. Indeed, the notion of counting and the notion of a sequence are intimately linked. Put another way, when we count out loud, each number must appear in a specific place in the sequence; it's not random. In a sequence, once a first term, always a first term. (*First* and the *fore-* of *foremost*, as well as *prime, proto-,* and the *-per* of Latin *semper* 'always, ever' all come from an Indo-European prepositional root, **per-*, meaning 'forward, through' and, by extension, 'first, early, before.') So place-in-sequence names (*first, second, third,* etc.—the *ordinal* numbers), like their quantitative counterparts (*one, two, three,* etc.—the *cardinal* numbers), are a necessity, not just an intellectual luxury.

The early Greeks, curiously enough, tended to exclude *one* from the thoroughfare, considering it not to be a number at all, but rather the unity from which all numbers are born. Perhaps they took the connection between numbers and sequence a little too seriously: How can you arrange one thing in a sequence? If there is only one thing there, you do not need a number to describe it. (We may smile at this until we recall our own expression *a number of . . .,* by which we invariably mean more than one.)

But *one* needs to be recognized as a number; otherwise certain operations do not make sense. (Plutarch was one Greek who acknowledged *one*'s numberhood: "We call unity a number, it being the smallest number and the first.") For example, the operation of addition takes two numbers and produces a third. 12 + 1 is a perfectly valid addition, whose first operand is *twelve* and whose second operand is *one*. Because the operands of addition must be numbers, *one* has to be a number for *twelve plus one* to make any sense—how else would anybody have known how many places to set for the Last Supper?

It was not until 1889 that Giuseppe Peano rigorously laid out the numerical highway, including 0 and 1, with a set of five axioms now known as the *Peano postulates*. The Peano postulates formally articulate the notion of numbers as a sequence. For starters:

1. 0 is a number (although not, technically speaking, a *natural number,* the lowest of which is 1).
2. If *x* is a number, then the successor of *x* (that number which

immediately follows x in the sequence, which, from now on, we'll write x_s) is also a number.

3. Any set satisfying clause one (that is, any set including 0) and clause two (that is, any set including any of its members' successors) includes all the natural numbers plus 0. (This one is slightly more difficult to grasp. It says that the "successorship path" defined by clauses one and two, beyond merely containing *only* natural numbers plus 0, also contains *all* the natural numbers. That is, if n is a natural number, it appears somewhere along the successorship path laid out by clauses one and two. One ramification of clause three: ½ is not a natural number, because the first two clauses do not provide a way to generate ½.)

Clauses one, two, and three are a somewhat naïve definition of the natural numbers; there are some flaws. The natural numbers plus zero can be characterized as being along a number line, so the structure we want is something like this:

Figure 1: The Number Line

$$0 \longrightarrow 0_s \longrightarrow 0_{ss} \longrightarrow 0_{sss} \longrightarrow$$

A number's successor is to the right of the number itself. In the diagram, 0_s equals 1, 0_{ss} equals 2, and so on.

The structure in Figure 1 satisfies the definition in clauses one, two, and three, but there are also some other structures that satisfy the clauses. Consider the following structure, in which 0 is its own successor:

Figure 2: Zero Succeeds Itself

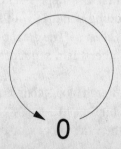

So we'll add a clause four: 0 is not the successor of itself or of any natural number. This eliminates the unwanted structure in Figure 2, but it still allows the following structure, in which 0 and each natural number has two successors:

Figure 3: Two Successors Each

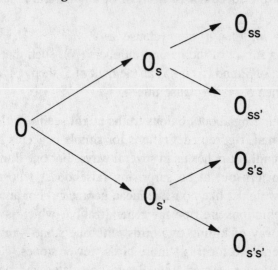

To solve this problem, we need a clause five: Each natural number or 0 has exactly one successor. This clause eliminates the unwanted structure in Figure 3, but it still allows the following structure, in which a natural number has two predecessors:

Figure 4: Two Predecessors

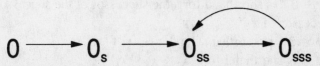

Figure 4 describes a structure in which two natural numbers, 1 and 3, share a successor, 2. So we need to add a clause six: A natural number can have at most one predecessor.

The naïve definition (clauses one, two, and three) plus the three amendments (clauses four, five, and six) make up the Peano postulates. Recapping, the Peano postulates are:

- 0 is a number (clause one).
- For each number n, there exists exactly one natural number n_s, which we call the successor of n (clauses two and five combined).
- 0 is not the successor of itself or of any natural number (clause four).
- If $n_s = m_s$, then $n = m$ (clause six).
- If S is a subset of the natural numbers (N), such that (i) 0 is an element of S, and (ii) if n is an element of S, then n_s is an element of S, then $S = N$ (clause three).

Such blathering about obvious truths might seem a little silly, but seeking formal, rigorous definitions for simple concepts like "number" profoundly enriches us in several ways. For one thing, obvious truths often turn out to be surprising falsehoods, whose exposure leads to new fields, like non-Euclidean geometry. For another thing, rigorous definitions are ripe for generalization, which is the mathematician's way of killing two birds with one stone—an expression whose generalized form is "more birds, fewer stones."

Mathematicians, armed with Peano postulates and possessing a nose for general patterns, have followed it to an appreciation of the essential nature of operations like addition, multiplication, and exponentiation: Each operation is shorthand for a more primitive and cumbersome cousin. Addition is a shorthand for counting; multiplication is a shorthand for repeated addition; and exponentiation is a shorthand for repeated multiplication.

- "$x + 3$" is shorthand for "the successor of the successor of the successor of x."
- "$x \times 3$" is shorthand for "$x + x + x$."
- "x^3" is shorthand for "$x \times x \times x$."

And if needed, there is another operation used as a shorthand for repeated exponentiations like the following:

$$X^{x^x}$$

Repeated exponentiation—called *tetration*—is so rare that a short-hand for it is hardly worth the trouble, appealing only to research mathematicians. Most professional engineers and scientists never encounter tetration, and the shorthand for it is seldom taught anywhere but in mathematics departments. But it doesn't stop there, and for the almost-unheard-of "multiple tetration" there is a yet stronger cousin operation, waiting in the wings.

All of which might have led Lao-Tzu to write:

> Counting gave birth to Addition,
> Addition gave birth to Multiplication,
> Multiplication gave birth to Exponentiation,
> Exponentiation gave birth to all the myriad operations.

For there *are* myriad mathematical operations—as many, in theory at least, as there are natural numbers—that can be derived as shorthand for their more primitive cousins. But that's a whole other story for another time.

TWO

OUR EQUAL, however lordly, is our peer; and two make a pair. Both *peer* and *pair* are from Latin *pār, paris* 'equal.'

For early Indo-Europeans, two was not just any number more than one, but a quantity that merited its own grammatical category—the dual. For example, if you were a Greek of Homer's day or a native speaker of Sanskrit and you felt called upon to remark that an ox was munching your apples, the verb for 'munch' would be singular; if a whole herd of oxen came stampeding through your orchard, they would do it in the plural. But if you yoked up two of them and began plowing your back forty, you would talk about those oxen in the dual, and the same went for anything in pairs, from a brace of cockerels to your neighbor's twins.

In Greek, a plural verb with a double subject signified that the agents were to be thought of as members of a larger class, rather than as a pair per se. So Xenophon uses a plural instead of a dual for the verb in the very first sentence of his *Anabasis,* where he tells us that the Persian king Darius and his queen, Parysatis, had two sons: an older one, Artaxerxes, and a younger, Cyrus. The plural verb is his way of letting us know, in passing, that the royal couple had other children as well.

In Latin, the dual eventually got phased out, its meaning absorbed into the plural, and the old dual forms were sent to the glue factory. (Exceptions that persisted for a very long time were *duo* 'two,' and *ambō* 'both.') This, indeed, was the model for the bulk of the other Indo-European languages as they evolved into their modern-day forms: We distinguish grammatically between the dichotomous singular and plural, but the notion of twoness still resonates strongly through our culture and the vocabulary that we use to express it.

Two is day and night, male and female, yang and yin, light and dark, right and wrong, right and left. We have two hands, two feet, two eyes, two ears, two lungs, two kidneys, and, depending on our sex, two ovaries or two testicles. This is no accident; even the simplest vertebrates exhibit bilateral symmetry, the appearance of the same thing on one side as on the other, only backwards. Our hands are mirror images of each other, though each hand by itself is not symmetrical: The only way to fit a left-handed glove on your right hand is to turn the glove inside out.

Mirrors fool us into thinking we see ourselves, when in fact what we see is exactly opposite. We are so used to this reversal that we can shave or tie a necktie in a mirror without a second thought. But try to shave the back of your own neck with a razor in one hand and a hand mirror in the other, reflecting off another mirror on the wall. Such a double reversal wreaks havoc with hand-eye coordination: One zigs when one should have zagged. Our favorite wise-guy answer to the age-old question, ''Why do mirrors reverse left and right, but not up and down?'' is ''Gravity.''

Human symmetry, though more than skin deep, is not total. We have but one heart, and it is not only asymmetrical but located slightly to the left of center—unless we are one of a pair of mirror twins, in which case it may turn up on the right. One of Lewis Carroll's eyes was distinctly lower than his other, and this, combined with his left-handedness, is said to have given rise to much of the play on reversals in *Through the Looking Glass*. As it turns out,

Alice does well to wonder whether "looking-glass milk" is good to drink; it probably isn't, for subatomic particles have their opposite antiparticles and when the two meet, they annihilate each other. Even if Alice and the glass of milk don't disappear in a white mist with red stripes, she mightn't find the milk particularly nourishing: Although complex protein and sugar molecules may exist in two possible mirror-image isomers, an enzyme or bacterium may break down only one of the two forms, leaving the other one untouched.

Left-handedness has a reputation in the West for being a bit sinister; in fact, *sinister* in Latin means 'left,' in opposition to *dexter* 'right.' Left-handers are a significant minority, somewhere between 15 and 30 percent of the population (depending on whose estimate you take). Most Romance words for 'right(-hand)' are derived from *dexter:* French *droit* means 'right' both in reference to direction and entitlement; Romanian *dreapta* means both 'right(-hand)' and 'correct;' Italian uses *destra* for 'right hand' and *destro* for English 'dexterous,' to which we may add *dextrose,* 'right sugar,' and *ambidextrous* 'equally handy with either hand' (but no *ambisinistrous* to signify 'equally clumsy with either'). But romance words for 'left(-hand)' are an odd lot: Spanish has *izquierda,* French *gauche,* Romanian *stang.* Even Latin couldn't make up its mind: In addition to *sinister,* the Romans used *laevus* and *scaevus.*

In China, left-handedness has no particularly negative connotations—except to Chinese Muslims, who (like all other adherents of Islam) regard the left hand as the unclean one, and will eat only with their right. In antiquity, the Chinese emperor's right-hand minister was always superior in rank to his left-hand one. But starting in the third century B.C., the left side of the emperor was considered the more honorable one when he received guests, because by that time it was his custom to hold audiences from a throne that faced south, east being considered an auspicious direction according to Chinese geomantic belief. For the same reason, the typical Chinese house was constructed along principles of auspicious orientation, so that a householder would normally sit on the eastern side of its hall, with his wife on the right side (that is, to his west), whereas in bed she lay on his left. And in the street—an area whose overriding principle was thought to be yin, i.e., female—the man walked on the right, the woman on the left.

Chinese is written vertically starting at the top right. Many other scripts read from left to right, inconvenient to left-handed people who must contort the writing hand to avoid dragging a sleeve in fresh ink. In Japan, one simply learns to write with the right hand even if one is left-handed, and that ends the matter. Though Westerners have a little more leeway in this regard, many of our tools (and weapons) only work properly in the right hand, and despite a few left-handed devices now on the market, most southpaws have grown up using right-handed scissors and aren't about to change now.

Left-handedness is associated with right-hemisphere dominance in the brain. Although the two hemispheres are interconnected through a vast net of circuitry in the corpus callosum, recurrent grand mal seizures in epileptics have sometimes led surgeons to sever these connections as a last resort. Two brain researchers, R. W. Sperry and Michael S. Gazzaniga, reported in the early 1960s that both hemispheres of such patients continue to function quite independently.

Our left hemispheres have a corner on language and logic, so right-handedness tends to be accompanied by a rational, analytic worldview. By contrast, the left-handed tend to have an easier time viewing things in holistic terms, have better spatial perception, and recognize objects more easily—and are more likely to draw them as they are, rather than "the way they're supposed to be." All children seem to have this ability to some extent, but most appear to lose it by adolescence, a time during which a fair amount of hard-wiring seems to happen in the brain. Even strongly right-handed adults, however, can learn to draw (again) by coaxing their right hemispheres into the partnership, as Betty Edwards's excellent book *Drawing on the Right Side of the Brain* demonstrates; one of her techniques is to sketch things upside down, so that their line and form predominate, and our eyes are not subverted by the tyrannical left brain's attempts to "make sense" of what we see.

It is not clear why our brains should be bicameral, but in general having two of something—kidneys, lungs, etc.—gives us some backup in case one of these vital organs decides to call it quits. Two eyes have the additional merit of establishing depth perception through parallax, which, when you close first one eye and then the other, is what makes nearby objects shift their orientation relative to the background. This advantage, however, is lost on many animals—e.g., ungulates like the caribou, whose eyes, on either side of their heads, result in separate visual inputs that their brains process independently.

Seeing double, of course, is a classic metaphor for visual derangement; but it is perhaps a testimony to the tenacity of dualistic thought that so many Western countries have legends about the Doppelgänger. It is incredibly bad luck for you to meet this double of yourself (and probably not so great for him or her either). Twins, on the other hand, seem to have an aura of the magical throughout the West: Jacob and Esau, Romulus and Remus, Castor and Pollux, Cautes and Cautopates (the attendants of Mithras)—all the way to Hansel and Gretel, who are dizygotic twins, that is, from two different eggs that happened to be fertilized at the same time. Though opposite-sex twins are always dizygotic, same-sex twins may be either monozygotic or dizygotic—that is, identical or fraternal. Folklorists and psychologists have suggested that mythical twins—particularly those with phonetically similar names like Romulus and Remus—were originally double aspects of a single person.

The Romans decided that the best way to prevent tyranny by one king was to have double chief executives instead. For almost five hundred years, from the expulsion of Tarquin the Proud to Marc Antony's defeat by Augustus Caesar, this seemed to work pretty well, except when the two *consulēs,* each of whom commanded an army in time of war, combined forces, in which case each consul served as commander in chief on alternate days. Differences in strategic philosophy could have disastrous consequences. When it was his turn to command at Cannae, during the war with Hannibal, the bolder of the two consuls (Gaius Terentius Varro) led his more cautious colleague (Lucius Aemilius Paullus) out of camp to get wasted along with most of both consular armies. (Varro himself, ironically, was one of the seventy Romans who survived the day.) At times like this the Senate, reverting to unitary thinking, would choose a dictator to straighten the mess out; the appointee would be given extraordinary powers for a strictly limited term of six months. One of these dictators, Lucius Quinctius Cincinnatus, who in 458 B.C. defeated the Aequians in just fifteen days and then promptly went back to his farm, was held up to Roman society as a model of civic temperance.

The military flaw in the consular system may have been that the partners truly were equal, whereas armies (and imperial bureaucracies) work hierarchically. The disintegrating Roman republic eventually saw its consular government give way to a series of dictatorships, punctuated by a couple of triumvirates in which the elimination of the weaker third man was inevitably followed by civil war between dueling generals. (Latin *duellum* 'duel' is unrelated to *dual*; it is, rather, a variant of *bellum* 'war,' the latter being an example of the same sort of phonetic shift that produced the *bi-* of *binary* from the Indo-European root for 'two'—**duo-/*dwi-*.) So a dual executive, originally a feature of Roman government that fostered stability, proved horribly destabilizing in the end, by which time most Roman citizens welcomed rule by an emperor as the price of putting a stop to the bloodshed.

Although Camille Paglia's study of Western sexuality, *Sexual Personae*, makes much of the transvestite pairings in Elizabethan drama, the tradition of mistaken identities actually goes all the way back to Roman comedy and to late Greek models before it. *Menaechmi*, the model for Shakespeare's *A Comedy of Errors*, is perhaps the most enduring of the comedies of Plautus. In *Amphitryon*, Plautus spins a fine tale of how Jupiter and Mercury came down to earth and fooled everybody into thinking that the two were the title character and his slave Sosia home early from the wars. Not the least of the fun is that the same two actors play the four parts. Even today, a mental disorder characterized by the erroneous belief that a person one knows is not that person at all, but someone doing a wickedly clever impersonation instead, is called the *illusion des Sosies* after Amphitryon's comic manservant.

The master-servant duo in drama itself also has a long pedigree, the servant usually being the more interesting member of the pair.

Jonathan, the comic-Yankee "waiter" in Royall Tyler's *The Contrast* (which, in 1787, was the first play in English to be offered in America by a company of professional actors) exemplifies this scenario. Here the servant has become a spokesman for social equality and the subversion of aristocracy. Figaro's similar political persuasions as the Count of Almaviva's servant in Beaumarchais's *Le Mariage de Figaro* (premiered in 1784) caused the play to be banned in France until the twilight of the old regime.

The sidekick of twentieth-century American popular culture seems made of different stuff. In contrast to the hero, who has typically been an intrepid, honest, somewhat humorless, and often not-overbright white male, the sidekick has typically been a person socially stigmatized in one way or another, whether by being black, Native American, foreign, a child, a woman, an oaf, or physically handicapped. Thus Batman's tireless fight against crime was assisted by the Boy Wonder, Robin; the Lone Ranger had his faithful Indian companion, Tonto (whose name in Spanish means 'stupid'); and the Cisco Kid roamed the West accompanied by the overweight buffoon Pancho. The hero often has a double identity as well—one as hero, frequently masked or otherwise outlandishly costumed, and the other as ordinary Joe, the hero's presentation of self in everyday life.

Interpretations of the true meaning of the hero-sidekick relationship abound. Is it significant that both Cisco and Pancho are diminutives for the same name (*Francisco*)? Again, the physical subtext may be the splitting of a single protagonist into the heroic (essentially tragic) and loutish (hence comical) components in us all; while we would all like to be capable of heroism, we really identify with the flawed, fallible buddy.

It has been said that the world is divided up into those who divide the world up in two and those who don't. George Carlin, a member of the latter group, rejects the dichotomy of the glass as half empty or half full, instead asserting a third possibility: The glass is too large. Most of the rest of us, however, exist comfortably (or, if you buy Woody Allen's assessment of life as consisting of "the horrible and the miserable," not so comfortably) in the former group, casually seasoning our everyday speech with such dichotomizing metaphors as "win or lose," "Jekyll and Hyde," "find oneself on the horns of a dilemma" (of which there are by definition two), "see in terms of black and white," "as different as night and day," and "off and on," the mother of all computer-science metaphors.

Computers are essentially boxes full of interconnected switches, each of which has two positions: on and off. In the first computers, built just after World War II, the switches had vacuum tubes; if there was current flowing, the tubes lit up, and if it wasn't, they didn't. This was not foolproof since sometimes a tube would burn out and not light even if the current was flowing. As a result, there was a limit to the size of such computers, since once there were a certain number of tubes, the probability that at least one of them would burn out at any given point approached certainty.

During the 1950s, however, William Bradford Shockley figured out how to make a smaller, more reliable switch by exploiting the semiconductor property of elements like germanium. A germanium diode acts like a resistor when a very small amount of current is put through it, but when the level crosses a certain threshold, the element undergoes a quantum jump (that is, its electrons leap up to a higher energy state) and will conduct electricity just fine. Now it became possible to measure, not the difference between full power and no power, but between high power and low power.

Shockley's innovation made vacuum tubes obsolescent if not obsolete and fathered, among other technological progeny, a whole new generation of portable AM radios. The transistor revolution, as luck would have it, coincided with the explosion of popular music in the late 1950s from its country-western and rhythm-and-blues antecedents—which angry parents exhorted their music-loving offspring to turn *off!*

"On" and "Off" can be represented by 1 and 0. These two numbers suffice for any arithmetical calculations one may wish to do, providing one is willing to do them in base 2. Our normal everyday calculations are carried out in base 10: We have ten numerals representing different quantities (including no quantity at all) and place notation means that when we get to ten we start over at zero in the units place and put a one in the tens place, to indicate that this is really zero-plus-ten rather than simply zero. Again, when we are talking about larger quantities, we may reckon by tens, tens of tens (i.e., hundreds), tens of tens of tens (i.e., thousands) and so on. As a result, we can theoretically express numbers of any quantity using just the ten Arabic numerals.

In base 2, instead of units (i.e., 10^0s), tens (i.e., 10^1s), hundreds (i.e., 10^2s), thousands (i.e., 10^3s), we reckon by units (i.e., 2^0s), twos (i.e., 2^1s), fours (i.e., 2^2s), eights (2^3s), sixteens (2^4s) , thirty-twos (2^5s), and so on. The arithmetic operations of base 2 are no different from those of base 10: The only difference is how we "spell" the quantity that we are trying to express. Here are how some base 10 numbers look in base 2:

Base 10	Base 2
0	0
1	1
2	10
3	11
4	100
5	101
8	1000
9	1001
11	1011
19	10011
69	1000101
525	1000001101

There are other bases possible besides base 10 (decimal) and base 2 (binary)—as many as there are whole numbers, really, though only a handful of these actually get used for practical purposes. Some American schools use base 5 to teach children about the nuts and bolts of arithmetic, because the small change of American currency (pennies, nickels, and quarters) provides a familiar and tangible set of pegs on which to hang the concepts of power and place—a penny, a nickel, and a quarter represent different powers of five (5^0, 5^1, and 5^2, respectively). You can collect any amount up to $1.24 with at most four of each coin. (Four is the limit because four is the highest numeral in base 5.)

Base 10	Base 5	Coins
4	4	4 pennies
5	10	1 nickel (and 0 pennies)
6	11	1 nickel, 1 penny
19	34	3 nickels, 4 pennies
20	40	4 nickels
21	41	4 nickels, 1 penny
24	44	4 nickels, 4 pennies
25	100	1 quarter
26	101	1 quarter, 1 penny
99	344	3 quarters, 4 nickels, 4 pennies
100	400	4 quarters
101	401	4 quarters, 1 penny
123	443	4 quarters, 4 nickels, 3 pennies
124	444	4 quarters, 4 nickels, 4 pennies

In a system with few numerals, large numbers take more ink: A two-digit decimal number might translate to a three-digit base 5 number or a seven-digit binary number (e.g., $99_{decimal} = 344_{base5} = 1100011_{binary}$, or, in standard mathematical notation, $99_{10} = 344_5 = 1100011_2$).

The number of digits required to express a given quantity in base 2 seems unwieldy to us, but computers are immune to tedium, and work very fast besides. (In computer terminology, a base 2 digit— i.e., the 1's place, the 2's place, the 4's place, and so on—is known as a *bit,* a contraction of *binary digit.*) Except for very large quantities or very complex operations, once a set of figures and calculation commands are entered into a computer, far more running time is devoted to turning the numbers from our base 10 input into base 2, which computers use, and to translating the answer back into base 10, than is spent on the actual arithmetic.

The electronic computation could, in theory, be just like the arithmetic we're accustomed to in the decimal system. Each base system has its own addition and multiplication table, but the mechanics of addition, subtraction, multiplication, and division do not vary. Addition, for example, includes the notion of "carrying over" digits from one column to the next, regardless of the base system you're using.

Furthermore, the quantities calculated by addition and multiplication are unaffected by base: Three times four is a dozen, whether you perform the calculation in decimal (i.e., $3 \times 4 = 12$), base 5 (i.e., $3_{base5} \times 4_{base5} = 22_{base5}$), or binary (i.e., $11_{binary} \times 100_{binary} = 1100_{binary}$).

And three *minus* four is negative one, regardless of base. The existence of negative numbers, every bit as possible in binary as in any other base system, requires an explicit rendering of the sign: positive or negative. But this is just another dichotomy, so computers can reserve within each number a special bit whose 1-or-0 (on-or-off) value indicates the number's sign. In such schemes, referred to as the *sign-magnitude representation* because the sign and magnitude are represented separately, computers use the leftmost bit to represent the sign ($0 = $ positive, $1 = $ negative). A computer with eight-bit sign-magnitude numbers uses only seven bits for each number's magnitude.

$$+5_{decimal} = 00000101_{8\text{-bit-sign-magnitude}}$$
$$-5_{decimal} = 10000101_{8\text{-bit-sign-magnitude}}$$

Adding two sign-magnitude numbers is simple: If both signs are the same, add both magnitudes and use the same sign in the result. If the signs differ, subtract the smaller magnitude from the larger and use the sign of the minuend.

Adding numbers with different signs—which entails a comparison to see which number is bigger, then subtracting, then adjusting the sign bit—is much slower than adding numbers with the same sign. "Smart" computers therefore try to simplify matters by avoiding the digression into subtraction altogether, the solution being essentially to effect subtraction using exactly the same procedure as addition, which is possible because every subtraction has an equivalent addition:

$$x - y = x + (-y)$$

Nevertheless, designing a computer with identical addition and subtraction operations is no cakewalk. It goes beyond merely switching to a different base system, requiring an entirely new form of arithmetic.

General base systems like decimal, base 5, and binary are cousins, related because the general operations of addition, subtraction, multiplication, and division work similarly. Internal computer arithmetic systems, however, are alien because the very rules of arithmetic (e.g., how to add, subtract, and negate numbers) change. These alternate systems can defy our intuition. For example, one popular system called *one's complement arithmetic* employs separate representations for positive zero and negative zero. Nevertheless, virtually all of today's computers use one's complement or a variant, *two's complement*. However bizarre, each of these systems has an unassailable internal logic, and computer scientists insist that the use of these systems has nothing to do with the problem on your utility bill.

Or so we heard Pancho say to Cisco shortly before they got their night-school degrees in Computer Science, forsook acting for steadier work, and rode off into the Silicon Valley sunset.

THREE

IT IS THE MORNING after a late-season blizzard, and your car is stuck in the snow. Some passersby volunteer to help you dislodge it, and gang up on the back bumper. On the count of three, they all shove as hard as they can, and you are on your way.

Why the count of three? The interval between "One!" and "Two!" sets the rhythm; only now do you know how soon to expect "Three!" This convention is fixed into our minds at an early age so solidly that a wily pediatrician of our childhood would fool her hypodermic-shy young patients by telling them that she would inject the vaccine on the count of three, then stick the needle in on "Two!"

Three points determine a plane. Three is the smallest number of sides a polygon can have. Three particular sides will yield at most one possible triangle, as every carpenter knows. But if the triangle is the essence of stability in mechanics, it is also a notorious fount of social instability: Jealousy is crueler than the grave. A new wrinkle on the classic love triangle was Jean-Paul Sartre's vision of Hell in *No Exit:* The man finds the lesbian more interesting than the bimbo, whom the lesbian finds more interesting than the man (who is basically a jerk), a circular triangle, if you will.

Because male-female courtship is dualistic in structure, if "we two form a multitude," then three is indeed a crowd, as any couple comparing their home life before and after the arrival of that first baby can attest. And the best thing about having a three-year-old is that you have survived the Terrible Twos without committing mayhem against your child or yourself to the funny farm.

If, on the other hand, you have three children, much of their childhood may be spent ganging up two against one, the one being therefore called the *odd man out*. If they beat him up and he goes to the hospital, the admissions department will do *triage,* the rough sorting out of prospective patients into levels of care; this term came from French army field surgeries, and referred to the three-way division of casualties into (1) those whose injuries require no more than first aid, (2) those who, while wounded sufficiently to be hospitalized, will probably recover, and (3) those who are so badly hurt that they are sure to die anyway. Burns are called *first-, second-,* and *third-degree,* in increasing order of seriousness.

As Tad Tuleja observes in *Curious Customs,* until the invention of the TV dinner (first marketed by the C. A. Swanson company in 1953), family mealtime was a three-part ritual of preparation, consumption, and cleanup. All three stages enhanced family solidarity through shared activity and communication, promoting the cherished goal of domestic life that the fifties called ''togetherness.'' The advent of TV meant that families now ate dinner watching it, subverting the communal consumption phase.

The TV dinner made it possible to eliminate the preparatory and cleanup phases as well, including any family ''quality time'' that went with these activities. Nutritionally, the TV dinner was a logical extension of army canned rations and the box lunch. Sociologically, it made it possible for family members to get through an entire day without substantial social intercourse.

A vulgar term for the penis is ''third leg.'' In opposition to the bifurcated female organ, the male genital apparatus is tripartite; hence, in China, two is female (yin) and three is male (yang). However, the Chinese consider the triangle a female symbol, and relate it to the snake. In the Judeo-Christian tradition, Adam and Eve were doing just fine till their snake came along to make three; Christians argue that this made inevitable the three crosses that went up on Golgotha on Good Friday—and the Resurrection on the third day, if you count inclusively. The first Easter was followed seven weeks later by the first Whitsunday, when the Apostles began speaking in tongues and the faithful first acknowledged the third Person of a Trinity in which God is at once Father, Son, and Holy Spirit.

According to the Hindu creation story, Vishnu made a tripartite universe (Earth, *Antariksha*—literally, 'the intermediate dwelling place'—and Heaven) with three steps of his immense feet. Perhaps it should be no surprise that much other Indo-European folklore is structured in threes as well. There are three Billy-Goats Gruff, any number of tales of three brothers each of whom sets out to make his fortune, three forays by the Dancing Princesses through a magic wood to a fairy ball, three days to guess the name of Rumplestiltskin, three parts to the Riddle of the Sphinx, three purses of gold thrown through a window by Saint Nicholas as dowries for three maidens otherwise sure to become prostitutes, three wishes when you let the genie out of the bottle, three Fates, three Norns, three Gray Ladies who shared a single eye and a single tooth, three blind mice, three coins in the fountain. Lithuanian folktales conclude with the ritual formula, "Three apples fell from heaven: One for the teller, one for the hearer, and one for the whole world."

Humor with threes is a folk staple as well. A famous tavern sign reads "We three loggerheads be"; it shows two sots, the reader being the third. Three turns up in many jokes of the form "How many *x* does it take to do *y*?" Thus: How many Californians does it take to screw in a light bulb? Three: one to screw it in and two to share in the experience. Other jokes resemble tripartite folktales: A narrative describes an event that takes place twice with the same results, the punchline hanging on what happens the third time, a classic example of the genre being the following:

It is September and Fred has just joined the mathematics department as a junior faculty member. To help him feel at home, his office mate, Mary, invites him to accompany the group of math department regulars when they go out for their customary end-of-the-week beer at the local watering hole. Off they all go, and the conversation is animated and friendly. At one point, Ralph, the abstract algebraist, says, apparently out of the blue, "Forty-seven," at which the regulars laugh uproariously. Fred thinks that this is a bit bizarre but, what with being new to the crowd, says nothing. A bit later, another member of the group, again, apparently out of the blue, says, "Twenty-four," at which, again, everybody laughs wildly. His curiosity getting the better of him, Fred turns to Mary and asks what's going on. "Oh," she says, "well, you see, we've all been hanging out together for so long that by now we've all heard each other's jokes, so a couple of years ago, we decided to number them all. Now, when somebody wants to tell a joke, he or she simply says the joke's number and lets it go at that." Fred ponders this bit of information and, when there is a lull in the conversation, says, "Thirty-one." There is a dead silence, and then the conversation picks up again. Fred asks Mary why nobody laughed, to which she replies, "Some people just can't tell a joke." (Fittingly, this joke has two variants of which we are aware: When Fred says "Thirty-one," the assembled company laughs long and loud and with great gusto, various of the group being reduced to tears. When he expresses surprise to Mary that his joke had created such a stir, she replies (a) "They'd never heard it told so well" or (b) "They'd never heard that one before.")

The numbers 1, 2, 3 can often be taken as the beginning of a sequence, rather than as a complete series. Mathematically, a sequence can be any succession of terms:

$$1, 2, 3, 4, 5, 6, 7, 8, 9, 10, 11 \ldots$$
$$1, 1, 1, 1, 1, 1, 1, 1, 1 \ldots$$
$$0, 1, 2, 3, 4, 5, 6, 7 \ldots$$
$$2, 4, 6, 8, 10, 12 \ldots$$

Mathematicians distinguish between a *sequence* and a *series*, which is a sequence on which addition is being performed, such as summing all integers between 1 and 666. We shall be finicky and preserve the distinction in what follows, while recognizing that most of the time people use *sequence* and *series* more or less interchangeably.

For what it's worth, *sequence* is from the Latin *sequor*, a deponent verb (one with an active sense but a passive conjugation) meaning 'I follow.' The *secūtor* was the gladiator armed with sword and buckler whose job, as the name implied, was to chase after the *rētārius*, who was armed only with a net (*rēte*) and fisherman's trident (*tri-* 'three' plus *dens, dentis* 'tooth.' A two-pronged version of the trident was used by butchers, whence, by analogy, *bidentia* came to mean 'animals for slaughter.') *Sequor* is related to English *pursue, suitor, sect,* and *sign. Series,* on the other hand, is from Latin *serō* ('I join/link together') and may be related to our *sort* and *sorcerer.*

A sequence can be finite or infinite. One way of defining a finite sequence is to list every one of its terms. But to define an infinite sequence, the terms must be capable of being generated, in order, by some procedure with a predictable result for each place in the string.

An infinite series can have a finite sum. Thus, as the Greek philosopher Zeno discovered when he posed the famous problem of Achilles and the Tortoise (in which the tortoise gets a head start in the race against Achilles, the fastest human, and gets to win the race because, according to Zeno, if any spatial distance consists of an infinite number of contiguous points that one must traverse to get from here to there, if you stop however briefly at each point, even if you're a tortoise, you'll always be ahead of the guy behind you who also has to stop at each of those points, however briefly) the series

$$\tfrac{1}{2} + \tfrac{1}{4} + \tfrac{1}{8} + \tfrac{1}{16} + \ldots$$

adds up to 1 exactly! And while the series of all odd numbers $(1 + 3 + 5 + 7 + \ldots)$ is infinite, the sum of the first n odd numbers turns out to be n^2.

If we say "the sequence that goes '1, 2, 3 . . .,' " most people will think we refer to the natural numbers—the positive integers, for which the formula for the nth term is simply $(n \times 1)$. Three terms of a sequence often suffice to tell you what the generative rule is ("2, 4, 6 . . ." strongly suggests that the formula for the nth term is $2n$), even as three notes of a popular hit usually are enough to name that tune.

Sometimes, as the Bonzo Dog Band once remarked, the pattern is more obvious. On the other hand, the start of a sequence can cling to ambiguity in the absence of additional information. Without rhythm, how can one tell the beginning of "Over the Rainbow" from that of "Bali Hai"? Both start tonic-octave-seventh (as does the song about Jack Frost nipping at an open fire and chestnuts roasting on your nose).

In 1973, N. J. A. Sloane, a mathematician at the Bell Labs in Murray Hill, New Jersey, published *A Handbook of Integer Sequences*. It contains over 2,350 sequences, of which two hundred begin "1, 2, 3 . . .," and no fewer than eight share the first five terms "1, 2, 3, 5, 9 . . ."

Here are two sequences:

$$1, 2, 3, 4, 5, 6, 7, 8, 9, 10, 11, 12, 13, 14 \ldots$$
$$1, 2, 3, 4, 5, 6, 7, 8, 9, 11, 22, 33, 44, 55 \ldots$$

A glance at the first nine terms of either would suggest that we're dealing with the entire sequence of natural numbers; but the sequences diverge from the tenth term. In fact, the second is the subset of integers that are palindromes, reading the same backwards or forwards.

Two sequences with entirely different terms but the same rule for getting from the nth term to the next are as follows:

$$1, 2, 4, 8, 16, 32, 64 \ldots$$
$$3, 6, 12, 24, 48, 96, 192 \ldots$$

For both, the rule is that the nth term is double its predecessor; only the starting places are different. In this case, we can generate the second sequence from the first: The nth term in the lower sequence is three times the nth term in the upper one. This is an example of a simple mapping rule that can be used to measure the relative sizes of two sets.

Often, the procedure that defines a sequence, finite or infinite, is an analytical expression: For the perfect squares (1, 4, 9, 16, 25 . . .), the nth term will be n^2; for the powers of 2 (1, 2, 4, 8, 16 . . .) the nth term is 2^{n-1}; for the positive odd numbers (1, 3, 5, 7, 9, 11 . . .) the nth term is $2n - 1$. But sometimes the defining law of a sequence can't be given by a simple analytical expression; instead, you must use a *recurrence relation*, which defines a term according to one or more of its predecessors. A recurrence relation (sometimes called a recursive definition) must explicitly declare values for some term or terms at the beginning of the sequence that have no predecessors, or not enough of them to kick in the recurrence rule. A classic example is named for the same man who argued for the adoption of Arabic numerals and made the case for decimalization four hundred years before it became fashionable, Leonardo of Pisa, a.k.a. Fibonacci.

A relatively obscure problem in Fibonacci's *Liber Abaci* caught the eye of the nineteenth-century French mathematician Edouard Lucas. We may call it the "Bunny Problem," which Fibonacci poses as follows: If you have a month-old pair of rabbits (one of each sex) who are currently too young to produce offspring, but during the second month and each month thereafter will produce another pair (again, one of each sex), and each of those pairs first begins reproducing during its second month at the same rate (of one pair per month), how many pairs are there at the start of each month?

It was Lucas who dubbed the answer the Fibonacci numbers. As can be shown empirically, they start like this:

$$1, 1, 2, 3, 5, 8, 13, 21, 34, 55, 89, 144 \ldots$$

At the start of the first month, there is one pair, the first term is 1. At the start of the second month, only that pair exists; the second term is also 1. Because the second pair arrives *during* the second month, there are two pairs at the *start* of the third month; the third term is 2. During the third month, only one of the two pairs is fertile, so only one pair is added; there are three pairs at the start of the fourth month, and the fourth term is 3. During the fourth month, two of the three pairs reproduce, so the fifth term is 5. And so on . . .

Each term of the Fibonacci sequence is the sum of the two terms preceding it. If we consider the first term to be 1, and the second to be 1, then when n is greater than 2, the nth term in the Fibonacci sequence is equal to the $(n-1)$th term plus the $(n-2)$th term—the third term (2) is equal to the second term (1) plus the first term (1);

the fourth (3) is equal to the third (2) plus the second (1), and so on.

The Fibonacci numbers can also be used to write a sequence of fractions such that the numerator of each is the denominator of the one immediately before it:

$$\tfrac{1}{1}, \ \tfrac{1}{2}, \ \tfrac{2}{3}, \ \tfrac{3}{5}, \ \tfrac{5}{8}, \ \tfrac{8}{13}, \ \tfrac{13}{21} \ldots$$

Successive fractions in this sequence get closer and closer to the *Divine Proportion* (whose symbol is the Greek letter phi, φ), which tells you where, on a line between points A and C, you must put point B, such that the ratio of lengths BC:AB will be the same as AB:AC.

Figure 5: Golden Rectangle

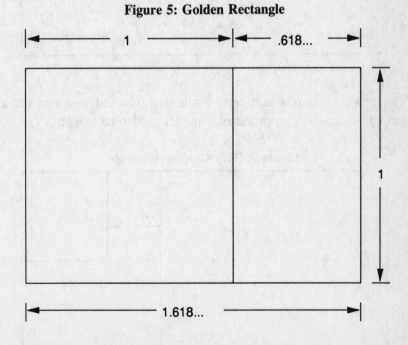

Golden Rectangles, whose short and long sides stand in this proportion, have permeated Western art from the Greeks on, and art theorists refer to their use as the principle of "dynamic symmetry."

Because its sides are in this proportion, the golden rectangle can be divided into a square and another smaller golden rectangle.

Figure 6: Little Golden Rectangle

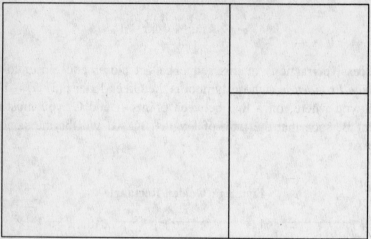

The process extends infinitely. Each time you cut a square off a golden rectangle, you produce a smaller golden rectangle.

Figure 7: Tiny Golden Rectangle

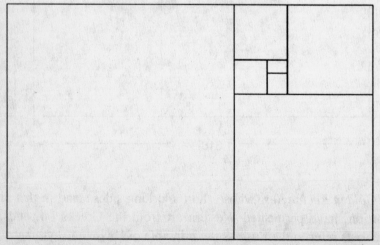

A *Handbook of Integer Sequences* includes, as a companion to the Fibonacci numbers, an entry for the *"tri*bonacci numbers," a sequence in which the *n*th number is the sum of the three terms preceding it:

$$1, 1, 2, 4, 7, 13, 24, 44, 81, 149, 274, 504, 927 \ldots$$

Sloane's catalogue also lists the "tetranacci numbers," each made by adding the preceding four terms (1, 1, 2, 4, 8, 15, 29, 56, 108, 208 . . .), the "pentanacci numbers," and the "hexanacci numbers" (the sums of the preceding five and six terms, respectively).

An example of a sequence that does *not* fall out from a simple (or even not-so-simple) expression, recursive or nonrecursive, is the set of *primes*—those numbers that are indivisible by any whole number other than 1 and themselves. (The fancy way of saying this is that each has no factors, or aliquot parts, other than itself and, for what it's worth, 1.) The number 3 is second in this sequence, which begins

$$2, 3, 5, 7, 11, 13, 17, 19 \ldots$$

Like the noble gases (helium, neon, argon, krypton, xenon, and radon), primes exist in splendid isolation; conversely, any *composite* number is the product of a unique set of prime factors. (Etymologically, a *composite* number is one that is put together from spare parts, i.e., factors other than itself or the unity, while a prime number is, literally, a "first"—an "original," we might say.) Thus, the prime factorization of 17 yields 17, while the prime factors of 60, say, are 2, 2, 3, and 5.

Are there an infinite number of primes? Yes, and you can easily prove it. If you multiply the entire sequence together up through the largest prime you know (call it *p*) and then add 1 to that product, it is clear that no matter which of the known primes you divide this new number by, there will always be a remainder of 1, and therefore that the new number must have a prime factor larger than *p; p* is not, therefore, the largest prime. (But this is *not* the same as saying that for any n, n factorial plus 1 will be prime, for $4! + 1 = 25 = 5^2$, $5! + 1 = 121 = 11^2$, and $6! + 1 = 721 = 7 \times 103$.)

The simplest means of generating primes with certainty is Eratosthenes's sieve, but this method is as tedious as it is exhaustive. How handy it would be to have shortcuts that would test very large numbers for primeness, or at least a formula that would give you a prime as the answer every time. *Mersenne primes* are a whack at the latter. Father Marin Mersenne was a friend of Descartes (they had been fellow students at the Jesuit college), knew Pascal and Fermat as well, and used to try problems out on all three of them. Mersenne was also a natural philosopher, a music theorist, and a theologian. His published works included the 1644 *Cogitata Physico-Mathematica,* in which he discussed numbers of the form $2^n - 1$ (now called the Mersenne numbers and represented as M_n, e.g., $M_4 = 2^4 - 1 = 15$). Mersenne said that the only values of n for which $2^n - 1$ is prime are given by the sequence 1, 2, 3, 5, 7, 13, 17, 19, 31, 67, 127, 257 . . . ($M_1 = 2^1 - 1 = 1$, $M_2 = 2^2 - 1 = 3$, $M_3 = 2^3 - 1 = 7$, and so on).

The function soon generates some very large numbers, and perhaps Mersenne is to be forgiven if he got some of them wrong. $2^{67} - 1$ isn't prime, but $2^{61} - 1$ is. (Historians of mathematics suggest that this was a misprint Mersenne failed to notice correct in galley proofs. Before typewriters became standard and authorial hardware, printers routinely set type from handwritten manuscripts, and errors were rife. With the advent of electronic typesetting, the opportunity for such mistakes has virtually been elimn8ted.) The highest number Mersenne reached, $2^{257} - 1$, turns out not to be prime either. And he missed a couple: $2^{89} - 1$ and $2^{107} - 1$.

Still, for an arithmetician with just pencil, paper, and perhaps an abacus at his disposal, Mersenne's accomplishment was nothing short of prodigious. On March 26, 1992, David Slowinski (working with rather more sophisticated tools) announced that he had found the thirty-second Mersenne prime. It is one less than a power of 2 that would take two hundred thousand digits to express.

Why is it so important to find primes, or to show that a certain integer is one? A very practical application in cryptography rests on the fact that since it is extremely hard to factor very large numbers, a two-hundred-digit number that was the product of two primes could govern text encoding: It would be virtually impossible to guess what the two numbers were if you didn't know them in advance, and out of the question (save perhaps on a state-of-the-art supercomputer) to go at it by trial and error.

Another sequence that is uniquely determined but lacks a quick-and-dirty algorithm:

$$3, 1, 4, 1, 5, 9, 2, 6 \ldots$$

These are the digits that make up pi (π), which is what you get when you divide a circle's circumference by its diameter. I Kings 7:23 implies that this ratio is simply 3, but Nehemiah, a rabbi and scholar working during the second century A.D., worked hard to show that the Bible did not contradict the Archimedean value (22/7) he knew about. The biblical passage describes a ''completely round'' molten sea ten cubits across and thirty cubits around. Nehemiah points out that a wall surrounds the circumference of this sea; if you measure the inner circumference but the *outer* diameter, the ratio could indeed work out to 3 exactly.

Ancient Babylonian texts vacillate between 3 and 3⅛, but π is in fact an irrational number, that is, a number that cannot be expressed as the *ratio* of one whole number to another or, put another way, as a whole-number fraction. (In Latin, *ratio* meant 'reckoning' in both the sense of 'computation' and 'reasoning,' the former being the meaning intended when referring to *rational* and *irrational* numbers.) There are, however, several series that *converge* on π:

$$\frac{\pi}{4} = 1 - \frac{1}{3} + \frac{1}{5} - \frac{1}{7} + \frac{1}{9} \ldots$$

(Leibniz)

$$\frac{\pi}{2} = \frac{2}{1} \times \frac{2}{3} \times \frac{4}{3} \times \frac{4}{5} \times \frac{6}{5} \ldots$$

(Wallis)

If you turn both sides of this equation upside down, you get

$$\frac{2}{\pi} = \frac{1}{2} \times \frac{3}{2} \times \frac{3}{4} \times \frac{5}{4} \times \frac{5}{6} \cdots$$

Count George Buffon, an eighteenth-century biologist who also translated Isaac Newton's work on calculus into French, showed that $\frac{2}{\pi}$ is also the probability that a needle, dropped from a height onto a grid of parallel lines exactly the needle's length apart, will land touching one of the lines.

Srinivasa Ramanujan (1887–1920), like Mozart, died brilliant and young, but not before making a permanent mark on his field. Ramanujan was a number theorist with a prodigious memory and astonishing intuitions, most of which proved correct when tested later on. He thought up several approximations for π, including

$$2\pi\sqrt{2} = \frac{99^2}{1103}$$

—accurate to eight places—and

$$\pi = \frac{63 \times (17 + 15\sqrt{5})}{25 \times (7 + 15\sqrt{5})}$$

—accurate to ten places!

The most remarkable chapter in the history of π is, in a manner of speaking, still being written. For *The New Yorker,* Richard Preston recently profiled two brothers in New York City, Gregory and David Chudnovsky, who have cobbled together their own personal super-computer out of mail-order electronic hardware. (It has more or less taken over Gregory's apartment near Columbia University, a fact that his wife and mother, who both live there too, accept with surprising good grace.) As of March 1992, the Chudnovsky brothers had managed to calculate π to 2¼ billion places, outstripping the billion and a half digits found by their only competitor, Yasumasa Kanada.

(Kanada held the world record as recently as 1986 with a mere 16 million places.)

While many mathematicians consider such an effort quixotic, Gregory and David Chudnovsky are looking for order in the seeming chaos of this irrational expansion. They hope that with enough numbers some pattern too subtle to see in shorter approximations of π will emerge. The running average of any string of π's decimal expansion is just above 4.5 for the first billion digits, and just under 4.5 for the second billion. Is this a hint of a pattern? Gregory Chudnovsky told Preston that it may be "close to the edge of significance." "We need a trillion digits," added his brother. And so they carry on.

FOUR

"AND AFTER ALL these things, I saw four angels standing on the four corners of the earth, holding onto the four winds so that no wind should blow on the earth or on the sea or on any tree." So wrote St. John the Divine, an octogenarian in exile on the mountainous island of Patmos, surrounded by miles and miles of the wine-dark Aegean Sea.

Like Aristotle five centuries before him, the author of Revelations would have seen ships disappear in the distance—first hulls, then decks, then masts—not simply vanishing to a point on the horizon. (The word *horizon* comes from a Greek verb meaning 'divide/separate,' e.g., by drawing a boundary line between, a *horos* being a 'boundary, limit, frontier.') Aristotle also pointed out that as one travels north, different constellations appear at the edge of the northern sky, which could not happen if the earth were flat.

Nor is it unthinkable that the Beloved Disciple knew about the Pythagoreans (who believed the earth to be a sphere for reasons both mathematical and aesthetic), or about Eratosthenes's measurements of noon shadows to guess (pretty accurately, as it turned out) the earth's circumference.

Eratosthenes was born about 273 B.C. in Cyrene on the North African coast, a hotbed of Hellenic humanism; he continued his studies at Athens with the heads of both the New Academy and the Lyceum. After a few of his literary and philosophical writings had circulated, he allowed himself to be recruited by the Egyptian civil service for duty in Alexandria, another great center of learning.

There, in the shadow of Alexandria's famous library, he worked faithfully for several of the Ptolemy kings. The library was already swelling, thanks to the confiscation and copying of any manuscripts visitors to Egypt arrived bearing. (The copies were later returned to the owners with the government's thanks, but the library retained the originals!)

Eratosthenes's first job was to teach young Ptolemy Philopator. Philopator grew up to be a diligent patron of the arts and sciences. At the age of forty Eratosthenes became chief librarian at Alexandria. This was an apt appointment, for Eratosthenes's learning was catholic and if it caused the envious to call him *Beta* ('Second stringer') and *Pentathlon* ('Jack of all trades and master of none'), as historian George Sarton says, "they proved their second-rateness and not his own."

In fact Eratosthenes's work in geography and geodesy was second to none. His calculation of the size of the earth was a typical mixture of his careful observation and clever reasoning. Eratosthenes knew of a deep well at Syene, upstream on the Nile, into whose depths the sun shone straight down at noon on the summer solstice, June 21. He believed that Syene was due south of Alexandria, and thought he knew how far south it was—five thousand *stadia*—both from estimates based on how far a camel could travel in a day and from an exact measurement paced off by a *bēmatistēs,* a surveyor trained to walk in equal steps and to count them. It remained only to measure the height of an obelisk and the length of its shadow at Alexandria at noon on the solstice.

His reasoning: At noon on the solstice the sun is directly overhead in Syene. In Alexandria, the sun is not directly overhead, but south of that—toward Syene. If Syene is nearby, the Alexandria sun is nearly overhead, but if Syene is farther south, the Alexandria sun is lower in the sky. If the sun is very low in the sky, the distance to Syene is a vast portion of the circumference of the earth. (If the sun appears on the southern horizon, for example, that means that a full quarter of the earth's circumference separates Syene from Alexandria.) So in Alexandria, he decided to measure what portion of a circle separates the sun from directly overhead.

Taking the obelisk and its shadow as two legs of a right triangle, Eratosthenes calculated the angle of the sun's rays at Alexandria. That angle, a little more than 7 degrees, represents a fiftieth of a circle, give or take. Thus, the distance between the well and the obelisk was approximately one fiftieth of the earth's circumference.

Eratosthenes's final modified estimate for the circumference of the earth: 252,000 *stadia*. The Greek *stadion* was equivalent to six hundred Greek feet or one hundred *orgyiai* of about 1.2 Roman *passūs* each—the *passus* (whence came English *pace* and *pass*) being the distance that one of your feet travels from when you pick it up to when you put it down again in a normal stride, which, by both Roman and English convention, measures roughly five feet. (*Passus* is from the verb *pandere* 'to stretch,' which comes from the same Indo-European root [*petH-*] that underlies English *fathom,* which originally referred to the distance encompassed by your outstretched arms. English *mile* comes from Latin *mille* [*passuum*] 'one thousand paces.') A *stadion* was a tidy length for a racecourse, including the one at Olympia (so named, and after it every stadium in the world). Harvard, when it built its pioneering reinforced-concrete football stadium at the turn of this century, made a somewhat pedantic point of making it a Greek *stadion* long. When we speak of something relative to "the length of a football stadium" we are unwittingly returning to this Greek unit of measurement.

However, there seem to have been multiple values for the *stadion,* depending where you lived. In Egypt, according to Pliny the Elder, 40 *stadia* = 1 *schoinos*, the *schoinos,* in turn, being 12,000 Egyptian cubits at 0.525 meters each. If so, Eratosthenes's 252,000-*stadia* figure works out to about 40,000 kilometers, compared to a figure of 46,000 if the Olympian *stadion* were used. But in any case the size Eratosthenes got was in the ballpark, and considerably better than Aristotle's earlier estimate of 64,000 kilometers. The actual circumference of the earth is quite close to 40,000 kilometers.

Furthermore, given the size of the earth, Eratosthenes thought he had the actual sizes of the moon and sun, thanks to an earlier calculation by Aristarchus of Samos showing their relative size to the earth. Aristarchus had realized that during a quarter moon (that is, when the moon appears half full) the sun, moon, and earth make a right triangle, with the right angle on the moon and the line from the earth to the sun the hypotenuse. (His reasoning: The sun shines directly on the moon. If it looks half full, we must be observing from directly off to one side.)

Earthbound, Aristarchus stood at one angle of a huge triangle, gazing into the sky at the other two. One angle (at the moon) is 90 degrees; another (at the earth) he measured by observing the angle between the moon and sun in the sky. Armed with two angles of a right triangle, Aristarchus calculated the third, and with that he calculated the proportions of the sides—the relative distances to the moon and to the sun.

Figure 8: Earth, Sun, Moon

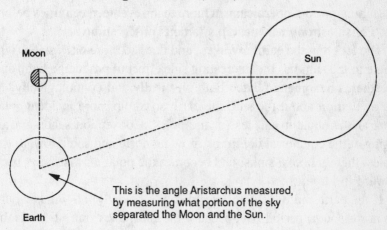

Moon

Sun

Earth

This is the angle Aristarchus measured, by measuring what portion of the sky separated the Moon and the Sun.

He figured the sun was about twenty times farther than the moon. He then figured that the diameters of the sun and moon were in the same ratio, because, despite the difference in their distances, they appear the same size in the sky: During a solar eclipse, the moon just blocks out the sun—no more, no less.

(Actually, these figures are very wrong; the sun is about four hundred times farther than the moon, but the mistake was one of measurement, not reasoning. He measured the angle between the sun and moon at 87 degrees; correct is about 89 degrees, 50 minutes.)

Coupled with some observations of lunar eclipses, and some more reckoning, he came up with a rough estimate: The moon is about one third the diameter of the earth and the sun is between six and seven times the diameter of the earth. These figures also suffered from measurement error, but were derived through flawless reasoning.

For all his observational floundering, Aristarchus seems to have had the stick by the right end. Eratosthenes's friend Archimedes, who may also have known Aristarchus personally, writes in his *Sand Reckoner* that Aristarchus modified these figures later in life, substituting for 87 degrees the much closer figure 89 degrees, 30 minutes—and, more astonishing, that Aristarchus argued for a cosmology in which the planets circled around the sun, and the earth's orbit bore "such a proportion to the distances of the fixed stars as the center of the sphere bears to its surface"—in effect, preaching proto-Copernicanism more than seventeen centuries before the Polish astronomer made his famous observations.

The fact that the earth revolves, and does so more or less at a right angle to the sun, has the interesting side effect of producing wind and weather, phenomena related both physically and etymologically. In its revolution about the sun, the earth soaks up more incident solar heat at the equator and less at the poles. Convection sends hot air rising at the equatorial doldrums, flowing north and south toward the poles; there it cools, sinks, and becomes the polar air that flows back toward the tropics.

If the earth did not rotate, or did so very slowly, all winds would be north-south, period. But because the earth does spin, the Coriolis force transforms this flow into a pattern of easterly trade winds (blowing from the southeast in the southern hemisphere and the northeast in the northern) to about 30 degrees south or north of the equator; from 30 degrees to 60 degrees the prevailing winds are from the west—blowing from the southwest in northern latitudes, and from the northwest in southern ones.

Eratosthenes also added four new names for winds from between the traditional four quarters, which the Greeks called *zephyros* '(north-) west wind'—probably related to *zophos* 'darkness, night' (compare German usage of *Abend* for both 'West' and 'evening')—

boreas 'north wind,' *notos* 'south(-west) wind' (not to be confused with *nothos* 'bastard,' a nickname of the Persian king Darius Ochus, whose son Cyrus hired ten thousand Greek mercenaries and raised the unsuccessful rebellion against his brother Artaxerxes Mnemon described in Xenophon's *Anabasis*), and *euros* '(south-)east wind,' possibly related to *eos* 'dawn,' but not, alas, to *Europe*—a place-name originally applied to Greece. Using *boreas* to designate the northeast wind, Eratosthenes called the true north wind *aparktikos* ('from the arctic'), and added *euronotos* for the southeast wind (from *euros* and *notos*), *argestēs* for the northwest wind (*argestēs* meant 'white, bright' and was originally an epithet associated with *zephyros,* because westerly winds cleared the sky of clouds), and *lips* for southwest (literally, 'a libation,' from *leibein* 'to pour forth').

The Romans adopted the Greek names for the winds more or less intact, though the north wind was also sometimes called *aquilo* (perhaps from *aquila* 'eagle' because its bite was so keen) and the south wind *auster* (a word for 'south' probably borrowed from Germanic, and originally meaning 'east,' being in fact cognate with Greek *euros*—compare the *Aust-* of *Austria*). For 'south(ern)' the Romans also used *merīdies* 'midday' (whence came English *meridian*), a contraction of *media* 'middle,' and *dies* 'day.' To this may be compared French *midi,* meaning both 'noon' and 'the southern part of France.'

English *south* is cognate with *sun*. Presumably the common denominator of south and the (midday) sun is heat; if mad dogs and Englishmen go out in it, the latter do so because the heat of noon is not all that warm in the British Isles. This brings to mind the story of the elderly British civil servant, cornered at an embassy party with a foreign diplomat. Grasping at conversational straws, the old imperialist says, "I hear in your country they worship the sun!"—to which the other fellow replies, "So would you Englishmen, if you ever saw it!" (Britons, in turn, are fond of making jokes about how lousy the weather is up north in Scotland.)

In some parts of the United States, *to go south* (elsewhere, *to go west*) can mean 'to die,' while *to go south with* something means to abscond with it, or to make it disappear. Presumably these are all related. For what it's worth, a number of Native American peoples believed that the south was the abode of departed spirits, which may have reinforced the more prosaic meaning that to go south of the Mexican border was to remove yourself from the jurisdiction of U.S. marshals. *Southpaw* ('left-handed') seems to have come from the fame of a particular left-handed pitcher—a rare and unsettling thing in early baseball—who happened to be from one of the states below the Mason–Dixon Line.

English *west* is cognate with Latin *vesper* 'evening'—whence came, of course, *vespers* 'evening church service,' one of the canonical hours in the Roman Catholic liturgy, the full set being *matins, lauds, prime, terce, sext, none, vespers,* and *compline*—if the middle four sound suspiciously like ordinal numbers, they mark the first, third, sixth and ninth hours after dawn, respectively. The Romans, though they called the west wind *zephyrus,* elsewhere used *occidēns* ('falling down,' i.e., of the sun) for 'west(-ern),' by analogy with their word for 'east(ern),' *oriēns* 'rising [of the sun]' (from the deponent verb *orirī* 'to rise').

Medieval European maps were "oriented" with east at the top. The convention of "north = top" came later, during the Age of Exploration, perhaps in recognition of the relative ease of unrolling a map side-to-side on a table, instead of scrolling it up or down.

When following a road map, north, south, east, and west may seem to us wholly arbitrary transformations of right, left, in front, and in back. But there is no denying the sun's apparent motion east to west, nor the floating needle pointing to the poles. Inhabitants of the Northern Hemisphere have always been able to look up at night and see the heavens appear to revolve about the aptly named Polaris, or the North Star, the bright star at the extreme end of Ursa Minor, the Little Dipper.

Curiously, it was the Big Dipper—Ursa Major—which the Romans referred to when talking about north as a direction: They called that constellation the Seven Oxen—the *Septentriōnēs,* of which the corresponding adjective, *septentriōnālis,* forms the basis in most Romance languages of the word for 'northern,' the word for 'north' in those languages being derived, typically, from the Germanic root that gives English *north*. It has been suggested that the underlying Indo-European root (**ner-*) meant something like 'under/on the left' (compare Oscan *nertro* 'left[-hand]'), here used in the specialized sense of 'on the left when you're looking east.'

So was St. John deliberately pulling our legs by describing an essentially flat, four-cornered, four-winded, and (by implication) rectilinear world, given the overwhelming evidence of the preceding centuries of Greek science against it? Not at all: Metaphoric and physical space can't always be mapped onto one another with 100 percent accuracy. And as a *metaphor* for the earth, the four-cornered plan was wholly comprehensible to St. John's contemporaries. Ancient China had imagined much the same thing: The world was a rectangle, like the interior of a carriage, while the heavens were a dome-shaped canopy above it.

Well, why not? The square and the right angle are, after all, essential parts of our rational understanding of the world. That most hyper-rational age, the eighteenth century, might be pardoned for introducing rectilinear street grids to the new cities of the New World. In 1811 a city commission in New York, intent on selling land efficiently, laid out the grid that fills up Manhattan north of Greenwich Village, reasoning that right-angled houses are easiest to build, and could fit most easily on right-angled lots. Washington, D.C. was planned according to a similar strategy, except that diagonal avenues were added, primarily with an eye to quick troop movements should the city ever require defense. (An added precaution: monumental statuary at major intersections to frustrate a straight shot down the boulevard by attackers' artillery; twenty-six-year-old Henry Knox had taken Trenton by the textbook strategy of posting a cannon on each road leading into town, then advancing while firing until everybody met in the town square.)

Thomas Hamilton, visiting Philadelphia from England in 1830, didn't care for the rectilinear look, calling it "mediocrity personified in brick and mortar. It is a city laid down by square and rule, a sort of habitable problem—a mathematical infringement on the rights of individual eccentricity—a rigid and prosaic despotism of right angles. . . ." But Ben Franklin, arriving seventy years earlier, thought it compared favorably to his native Boston, where making four right-hand turns in a row almost never brought one back to the same corner (and still doesn't to this day, with the added problem of going the wrong way down several one-way streets and, if one is riding a bicycle, risking one's life in the bargain).

There is something unsettling about buildings and human spaces that deliberately set out to negate the right angle. Not the least disturbing feature of the German Expressionist film classic *The Cabinet of Dr. Caligari* is its sets, which are deliberately constructed with false perspectives and peculiar angles. Shirley Jackson's story "The Haunting of Hill House" derived some of its aura of malaise from the absence of 90-degree angles in the building. (Overdoing rectilinearity can cause problems too: Sci-fi fans will fondly remember Robert Heinlein's 1950s yarn "And He Built a Crooked House," in which a madcap architect's home, designed to be an imitation of a hypercube, collapses into a true one as the result of an earthquake.) Subtler, perhaps, are the real-life Yale colleges named Stiles and Morse, designed by Eero Saarinen with rooms of irregular shape, some of which were so nonrectilinear that the only way a bed would fit in them was in the middle of the room.

It has been suggested that our fondness for the 90-degree angle is innate, a function of the profound extent to which we are characterized by bilateral symmetry (as opposed to the radial symmetry that characterizes the starfish and the sea urchin), which virtually obliges our bodies to be oriented in one direction or another at any given time, conscious of the distinction between front and back, left and right, and, of course, up and down.

(At certain colleges, oddly enough, freshman "orientation" weeks used to be characterized by great and general disorientation, exacerbated, no doubt, by the consumption of vast quantities of illicit alcohol, and symbolized by the compulsory wearing of the beanie, a hat distinguished by its radial symmetry.)

Every Navajo recognizes three-dimensional orientation; the devout address prayers to all six directions, even though able to travel in only four of them. (The wicked can travel in all six: Navajo witches, like European ones, are supposed to be able to fly.) But apart from

would-be witches and the occasional ornithopter crank, Europeans before the hot-air balloon left the sky alone: It was, after all, the ethereal
abode of spirits and was unattainable, at least during life, by ordinary
human beings—while the less said about down below the better.

Which brings us back to the ground zero or square one of terra
firma, where examples of right-angle imagery and metaphor have
been with us in abundance since well before the days of St. John: We
speak of quarter hours (never third hours, though twenty minutes
divide an hour as well as fifteen minutes do)—and *square* in contrast
to *hip*, although more recent usage has replaced *square* with *straight*,
now meaning 'unhip' and 'not stoned,' though formerly it was simply the opposite of *crooked*. *Rectitude, correctness, rectangle,* and
erection all come from Latin *rectus*, originally meaning 'straight,
(up)right,' which is from an Indo-European root (**reĝ-*) whose original sense of 'straight' lurks beneath the surface in English *rule,
regulate, reckon,* and *right*.

The Latin for 'a square' was *quadrum,* from *quattuor* 'four,' *quad-
rilaterus* being something of a linguistic afterthought (from *quadri-*
plus *latus* 'side') that the Romans used to describe a generic (not
necessarily square) four-sided figure. Perhaps with an eye to Greek
usage and to be on the safe side, the Romans also coined the term
quadriangulus 'having four angles' (from *quadri-* plus *angulus* 'angle, corner,' the term that appears in the Vulgate version of Revelations 7:1—*Post haec vidī quattuor angelōs stantēs super quattuor
angulōs terrae . . .*, which must have given the euphonious St. Jerome great pleasure to translate, given the fortuitous similarity in
sound of *angelus* 'angel' and *angulus* 'corner'). The English word
square comes from a late Latin compound *exquadrāre* 'to make
square,' also the basis for *squad(ron)*—a square formation of soldiers. This may be the basis for the English expression *square off*.
Foursquare (as in "Foursquare Gospel Church") originally meant
'simply but unassailably square,' later taking on the meaning of
'solid, reliable, steady.'

The Greek for 'square' was *tetragōnon*—*tetra-*'four' plus *gōnia*
'angle, corner.' The term for a quadrilateral was *tetrapleuron*—*tetra-*
plus *pleuron* 'side' (originally, 'rib,' whence came *pleurisy* 'pain in

the side')—which could include not only the square but the parallel-ogram and rhombus. A *rhombos* was originally a 'bull-roarer,' i.e., a wooden slat attached to a piece of string. Whirling the slat produces a buzzing noise. (*Rhombos* is related to the Greek verb *rhembein* 'to spin, turn round and round.') Bull-roarers had ritual uses in Greece, and the Romans borrowed the term *rhombus* to designate a similar instrument used in rites of magic. It is presumably from the diamond shape of the bull-roarer's slat that *rhombus* came to designate the geo-metrical figure. It is ultimately the magical aspect of the *rhombus,* according to the Spanish lexicographer Corominas, that underlies the use of the term *rhumba* (or *rumba*) for a dance of Cuban origin that, like the Argentine tango, was imported into American dance halls early in this century. The semantic route runs something like this: Just as English *prestige* is derived from a Latin term meaning 'illusion caused by magic,' so we might derive Spanish *rumbo* in its sense of 'pomp, ostentation' from *rhombus* in its sense of 'magical device,' sliding easily from 'ostentation' to 'provocative ostentation' to 'dis-turbance, disruption' to 'carousing' to 'provocative dance' with a trip to the Caribbean and a change in the noun's gender thrown in for free.

If deriving a two-dimensional quadrilateral (never mind a popular New World dance form) from a circular motion in the air involves a stretch of the imagination, consider the stretch that it takes to represent the spherical world on a flat surface, a challenge that has occupied mapmakers from time immemorial. This challenge has been met by the invention of a number of projection schemes, such as that of Mer-cator who first represented longitude as parallel vertical lines. No mat-ter that this projection ludicrously distorts land-mass sizes as they lie farther from the equator: On such a map, a constant compass heading (the easiest course for a ship's pilot to steer) translates into a straight line, called a *loxodrome* (from Greek *loxos* 'slanting' and *dromos* 'running course, racetrack') or, more commonly, a *rhumb line* (of which the *rhumb* portion is most plausibly to be derived from *rhombus* via Spanish *rumbo* in its sense of 'point of the compass, direction').

On the surface of a globe, however, it soon becomes apparent that an itinerary based on a constant compass setting is by no means the shortest trip. A typical constant compass heading is a spiral toward one of the poles. Airlines, for reasons of fuel economy, fly long trips along what are called *great circle* routes. On these routes, the same line if extended all the way around the globe would put you back where you started, passing through the most distant point of the world along the way. A flight from Quito, Peru, to Entebbe, Uganda, for example, would follow a *great circle* almost identical to the equator, one of the few trips one could plan with a Mercator projection and get a direct itinerary.

Other projections serve other ends. One common complaint about the Mercator projection is that it exaggerates Europe, Russia, and North America, while deflating the Third World. Arno Peters, a German historian, revived an equal-area projection first described in 1855 by a Scot, the Reverend James Gall, in which Africa and South America show pronounced vertical stretching, with the visual importance of the superpowers in respect to the rest of the world significantly diminished. A parodic response by U.S. Geological Survey cartographer John Snyder—an hourglass-shaped equal-area projection reducing the equator to a single point (thus showing that areal fidelity may not always go hand in hand with shape fidelity)—did not stop the Peters-Gall projection from finding much favor with certain agencies at the United Nations, as well as with the World Council of Churches and the Lutheran Church of America, all of whom had diplomatic or missionary interests of their own in the Third World.

For very short journeys, pilots needn't fuss with great circles or compass headings: They simply follow highways, railroads, or rivers, which is how Tom navigated from a hot-air balloon in *Tom Sawyer Abroad*. Like most navigators of his day, he also looked for major landmarks, including Illinois, which he expected to be pink because he had seen it that way on a map.

Cartographers have long known that color can be a powerful means of dramatizing the contents of a map, but it was only with the substantial advances in the technology of color printing in the nineteenth century that the use of color became feasible in mass-produced maps of the sort that Tom Sawyer might have seen (with Illinois in pink). Like most new technologies, the robust possibilities for color printing in cartography presented its users with a number of decisions critically affecting the intelligibility of the end product: As *The Macintosh User Interface Guidelines* puts it, color

allows us to "discriminate between different areas, . . . show relationships between things, [and] identify crucial features . . . [but]
the mind can only effectively follow four to seven color assign-
ments . . . at once."

In 1852, Francis Guthrie wrote a letter to his brother Frederick, a
student of the great logician Augustus De Morgan, in which he
conjectured that four colors should be sufficient to color any flat map
such that no adjacent regions of the map would be the same color,
and asked if Frederick knew of any mathematical proof of this con-
jecture. Frederick did not; nor did De Morgan; and for another 124
years neither did anyone else.

The four-color problem can be easily visualized: Look at central
Europe. Switzerland is bordered by France, Germany, Austria, Italy,
and Liechtenstein. Six colors? Not necessary, since France and
Liechtenstein, being noncontiguous, can be the same color, as can
Germany and Italy. Four colors suffice.

And "Four colors suffice" became the motto on the postage meter
at the university where Kenneth Appel and Wolfgang Haken solved
the problem in 1976. What was astounding about this proof was that
its rigor depended on number-crunching by computer: Appel and
Haken split the problem into about fifteen hundred smaller problems
and programmed their computer to solve every one of them. Many
mathematicians grumbled at this, since the usual way they solve
problems involves a sudden flash of insight, like the sound of a great
"Aha!" (Henri Poincaré's realization that certain transformations
used to define Fuchsian functions are identical to transformations
used in non-Euclidean geometry, which came to him as he was
stepping onto a streetcar, or Bertrand Russell's sudden insight, while
riding his bicycle down a country road, that he was no longer in love
with his wife). The four-color proof was hard to swallow because
there was no way to do so in a single gulp.

Of course, an atlas typically uses more than four colors anyway:
For one thing, just because a thing is possible doesn't mean that it is
easy; for another, water is almost always printed as blue, and land
isn't; and for a third, countries sometimes have noncontiguous ter-
ritories—e.g., Alaska plus the Lower Forty-eight, or Pakistan until
its eastern part seceded and became Bangladesh.

The four-color map theorem is an assertion about graph theory, which is the study of discrete points and the lines that connect them; each point is called a *vertex* and each line is called an *edge*. To convert a map into a graph, for example, we might mark the capital city of each country, and then draw lines connecting capitals of adjacent countries. Such a symbolic representation has real uses. A familiar version of a connect-the-cities graph, for example, can be found in any airline system route map, generally with flying times printed above each line.

A classic problem that yields nicely to graph theory is the "Seven Bridges of Königsburg"—nowadays called Kaliningrad, located on the Preger River some sixty miles to the east of Gdańsk, Poland, in what used to be part of East Prussia. Local folk had observed that when one tried to take a walk crossing each of the city's seven bridges (which connected both riverbanks with two islands in the middle of the stream), without crossing any bridge twice, there seemed to be no way to do it.

Figure 9

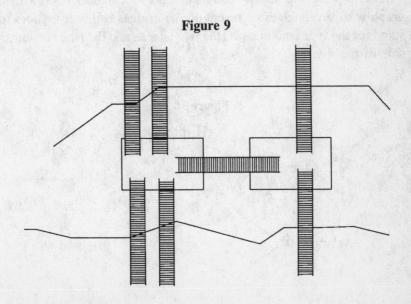

The Swiss mathematician Leonhard Euler realized that if a land mass has an even number of bridges, any walker crossing each bridge once will enter and exit the land mass an equal number of times. If an island, for example, has four bridges, you can cross two bridges while entering the island and two others while leaving it. If you start on the island, you will finish on it, and if you start elsewhere, you will finish elsewhere.

By contrast, if a land mass has an odd number of bridges, you cannot hope to return to your starting point if you plan to cross each bridge exactly once. For example, if you start a walk on a riverbank with three bridges, the first bridge takes you away, the second returns you, and the third takes you away again. Similarly, if you start a walk *elsewhere* from such a riverbank, your walk must end on that riverbank, because you will twice cross bridges toward the bank, but only once cross a bridge leaving it.

So if a walk includes a land mass with an odd number of bridges, that land mass must be either the starting point or ending point. But all Königsburg's land masses have an odd number of bridges, so you cannot walk through the city crossing each bridge exactly once.

Euler represented the city and its bridges schematically, drawing a graph with seven edges representing the bridges and four vertices to stand for the four land masses (the two islands and the lands on either side of the river).

Figure 10

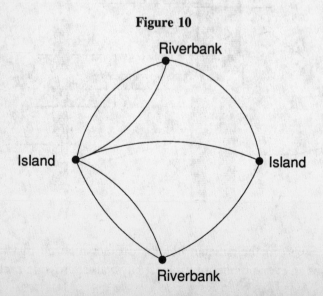

Euler's solution marked the beginning of graph theory, which has had some surprising applications since. For one thing, it can be used to prove that the number of people in history who have made love an odd number of times is even.

Consider a graph in which each vertex represents a person. Edges—the lines drawn between them—will represent acts of love-making. At first, the population consists of Adam and Eve; they make love, and we draw a line between those two points. Now Cain is born (dot #3). Adam and Eve make love again (a second line between dots 1 and 2) and Eve gives birth to Abel (dot #4). Cain's wife turns up from somewhere unspecified (#5), and behold, Cain knew his wife (draw an edge between dots 3 and 5). After a few generations of this, the map starts to look a bit complicated; those who make love a lot begin to look like major trade centers on a road map, while the utterly chaste remind one of unconnected outposts in the hinterlands.

The graph-theoretical assertion here: In any graph, the number of vertices with an odd number of edges is even. If one goes at it empirically, examining each vertex in turn and jotting down the number of edges, the total will be an even number. Why? Because each edge connects two vertices, and thus the total number will be double the number of edges, and multiples of two are by definition even. For every odd number in the list, there must be another odd number elsewhere in the list. Or, put in vernacular terms, it takes two to rhumba.

FIVE

"TAKE FIVE!" says the bandleader, and the musicians light up: Five minutes is the approximate time it takes to smoke a cigarette. Greek peasants, when asked how far it was to the next village, used to say "*n* cigarettes," *n* being equal to the number of cigarettes you'd have time to chain-smoke while walking the distance.

The connection between time elapsed and something burning at a constant rate is as old as the first incense clocks of China. The Chinese divided a day (reckoned midnight to midnight) into one hundred *k'o,* a unit equal to a little less than a quarter of a Western hour. In addition to sundials for daytime use, by 500 A.D. the Chinese had candles, water clocks, and incense sticks with which they measured the night watches; and in 1073 an imperial official named Mei-ch'i invented the "Hundred-K'o Incense Seal" (*pai-k'o hsiang-yin*) as a replacement for the water clock during a period of extreme drought.

The incense seal was a mazelike pattern of grooves into which the user would spoon incense; lighted at one end, it would slowly burn its way down the groove at a steady and known rate. Because the length of the night varies with the season, as many as thirteen different seals could be used depending on what time of year it was; and contemporary sources list over a dozen different recipes for horological incense.

Chinese timekeeping by fire was by no means a ruling-class prerogative; there was a "poor man's alarm clock" consisting of a length of punk cord with knots in it for so many *k'o* that, when stuck between the bare toes and lit, would burn down until the heat on the bare skin would awaken the sleeper (and perhaps everyone else in the house).

A classier version—described by the Jesuit Gabriel de Magalhaens, who visited China in 1668 and built several Western-style clocks for the emperor—was a coil of formed incense suspended over a brass pan; to this was attached a weight at the point on the coil corresponding to the number of *k'o* one wished to sleep. When the incense burned up to the weight, it would drop into the pan with a clang loud enough to wake anyone nearby.

Both matchcord and incense sticks were borrowed by the Japanese, who used the latter in geisha houses, where women used them to keep track of the time spent entertaining clients; so a geisha might say, "I earned six sticks yesterday!" This persisted well into the 1920s, and as recently as the 1950s the term *senko* ('incense stick') was still used figuratively to mean "half-hour of a geisha's services."

Time itself is smooth, continuous, flowing. We watch the shadow of a gnomon creep across the face of a sundial, the incense stick or candle slowly shrink, or water drip in steady rhythm into a basin. All but the first have the merit of working even when the sun is down or when the day is overcast.

Inside the courtrooms of Athens, the standard water clock (or *clepsydra,* literally 'water thief,' from the *klep-* that gives us *kleptomaniac* and the *hydr-* that gives us *hydraulic*) allowed six minutes for speaking; at Rome, it was closer to twenty. If time was needed to consult documents or to read them into the record, the speaker would ask that the upper vessel be stoppered for the moment. A Roman wit fancies that a certain long-winded lawyer, slaking his thirst from a water jug, might serve everyone better if he drank the contents of the water clock instead.

Great Moments in Clepsydra History: Ctesibius of Alexandria built a water clock with a flotation indicator in the second century B.C. Su Sung engineered a magnificent water clock for the emperor of China in the eleventh century A.D. (It also showed various celestial motions, the clock part being somewhat of a bonus: the emperor, for astrological reasons, was primarily interested in the motion of the sun, moon, planets, and stars.) The last serious geocentric astronomer, Tycho Brahe, used a clepsydra to time durations of celestial events.

But let us not slight sand in an hourglass. With a scythe, it has formed the two stock emblems of Father Time for the last five centuries. Sand clocks range from the dime-store three-minute egg timer to the multiton sandglass at the Sand Museum of Nima-Cho, Japan, which is turned once a year, the entire town pulling on the ropes. Although sand consists of discrete particles, they're so small that their aggregate behavior approximately obeys the rules of fluid dynamics.

Yet our most accurate timepieces tick rather than flow. Analog watches—those with a clock face—speak of the continuity of time; digital ones belie it. The hands on a clock face change smoothly, gradually, as time progresses. Digital watches subdivide time with a jolt, changing drastically from one instant to the next.

The difference between the smooth display of analog watches and the jerky ticks of digital ones illustrate the difference between what mathematicians call *continuous functions* and *noncontinuous functions*.

In mathematics, a *function* is a sort of converter: It converts a value to some other value. Typical is the square function, which converts numbers to their squares: If you feed 7 in, you get 49 out; likewise 5 in yields 25 out. A currency exchange rate is also a function: For the U.S.-to-Poland currency exchange, you feed in dollars, you get out zlotys.

Wristwatches are machines that calculate a function for us: They convert input (the time of day) to output (a visual display). From a mathematical point of view, a digital watch is a very different sort of function from an analog one. At various times 'round midnight, the various outputs of an analog watch look similar, whereas a digital watch's outputs look very different. In the one second between 11:59:59 and 12:00:00, almost every portion of the digital watch's (or converter's, or function's) output changes. The analog watch is more honest, because its display is every bit as smooth and continuous as time itself.

Paraphrased, the mathematical definition of a continuous function requires that any small change in the input will result in a small change to the output. At midnight, the digital watch severely violates this requirement, whereas the analog watch satisfies it gracefully: 11:59:59 on a clock face looks like midnight—"close enough for folk music."

Ironically, until the invention of electronic timepieces, the clock face's continuous display represented the conversion of an internal clockwork that relied on an escapement—a ratchet that would catch and then release a wheel powered by spring or weights in a series of discrete ticks and tocks registering the passage of time.

Galileo, it is said, first began thinking hard about the pendulum when he noticed an acolyte's censer swinging on chains at High Mass. Timing the swing with his pulse, Galileo realized that the frequency of the swing (i.e., how many times the thurible went back and forth in a given time) was independent of the amplitude (i.e., the distance of the swing from side to side). Further experiments would show that the frequency was dependent on the length of the chain.

Before then, clockwork escapements were tripped by a bar that rocked from side to side with a weight attached. But these lost time as they ran down and had to be readjusted frequently. The pendulum made it possible to build clocks that would run smoothly until they stopped, providing nobody jiggled them.

Nevertheless, Galileo resorted to a clepsydra to time experiments on acceleration, capturing the outflow of water from the device during several trials and weighing it, weight being the most precise form of measurement then possible.

Astronomers going all the way back to Babylon and Egypt have shown a keen interest in time. This is almost a tautology, since it is the apparent motion of the sun, moon, and other heavenly bodies that defines time for us: The sky is always right. If our calendars or clocks don't agree with it, we need to adjust them or redesign them until they do. Only with the advent of electronic watches, which count the vibrations of metal tuning forks or electrically excited crystals, has timekeeping become independent of the sky.

"What times does the sun rise?" is a modern question that puts the cart before the horse; for most of humanity throughout its history the standard answer has been, "The sun rises at sunrise," and that's that. Similarly, "When is midday?" has a conventional answer ("Noon") but that is only an approximation: Midday is the moment the sun reaches its maximum elevation during the day. Midday coincides with noon only a few times a year, and only on certain meridians, and only if you're not using local daylight saving time. In reality, noon is merely a time that is close to midday every day.

For the lay member—i.e., the nonastronomer—of an agrarian culture, *sunrise* was accurate enough as an expression of the time. The rising mercantile societies, however, required a more accurate expression of time for the general public because they needed cooperative scheduling. At first this was as simple as a bell that chimed the hour; the word *clock* originally meant 'bell.' *Punctuality*—being prompt to the minute—was not an issue until the late eighteenth century; it is conspicuously absent from Ben Franklin's famous list of twelve goals for his own improvement.

It could be argued that the very idea of punctuality, as we know it, had to wait until refinements in clockmaking made possible a portable watch with a minute hand. In any case, the demand for accurate time in smaller bites, once aroused, undoubtedly spurred the technology. There were life-and-death reasons too, mostly having to do with the longitude problem.

As Europe's trade routes grew, its mercantile civilization stretched beyond its local time zone. Latitude is easy to calculate, as Eratosthenes showed; the Renaissance mariner on the daytime high seas could measure the angle of elevation of the sun at midday and, in a day-by-day table showing the sun's declination, find out how far north or south his ship was from the sun. Nighttime calculation in the Northern Hemisphere was even easier, using Polaris.

Longitude is easy too, providing you have a clock that keeps time from where you set out. If you set your clock in London, and then sail to Sweden to observe the sun, at midday your clock will say 11:00 A.M. It is thus possible to calculate that you are about 15 degrees east of where you started (that is, one twenty-fourth of the full circumference of the earth). In fact, you can calculate your longitude precisely—but only if your clock has kept good time on the trip.

These fairly simple calculations turned out to be a great challenge to early clockmakers, however: The roll, pitch, and yaw of ocean travel threw clocks hopelessly out of whack when it didn't stop them altogether. Errors in longitude could be disastrous, as the British saw in 1707 when a fleet of their warships, commanded by the popular Sir Clowdisley Shovell, foundered off the Scilly Isles causing great loss of life: The crew had thought the islands well to their east.

The governments of Spain, the Netherlands, and France had all advertised large prizes for solutions to the longitude problem, but the British, in the wake of the accident above, offered the largest reward of all—twenty thousand pounds, along with stipends of a tenth that sum to support promising experiments. There was a sudden spurt in longitude research, much of it crackpot and inspiring many jokes: Hogarth's 1736 madhouse scene in the *Rake's Progress* series shows a lunatic trying to solve the longitude puzzle.

One of the candidates, John Harrison, won the prize in 1714 when his "model #4" clock passed the test set down by the British Board of Longitude: To make a trip to Jamaica (at that time a nine weeks' sail from England), and not lose more than forty seconds. Harrison's clock lost under six seconds, which converted to about a minute and a quarter of longitude, or a couple of miles—well within the thirty minutes of longitude specified by the board.

Harrison, son of a carpenter and a painstaking craftsman himself, used wooden gears (self-lubricating, thanks to natural oils) and added a balance spring to regulate the mainspring driving the works. Harrison's design did more than satisfy the demand for marine clocks. Although wearable clocks—watches—had been invented in Nuremberg around the beginning of the sixteenth century, they didn't keep very good time. Harrison's balance-spring innovation cured that, making possible a fashionable punctuality.

In America, the railroad and the Civil War were the two great stimuli to standardized time and universal watch ownership, for on the tracks and on the battlefield the failure to synchronize activities can get a lot of people killed. After enough spectacular "cornfield meet'' train collisions, the U.S. Congress was persuaded in 1883 to adopt standard time zones. The Waltham Watch Company got its big break with the call for cheap soldiers' watches for the Union army. Having a watch, of course, does not necessarily mean that it is synchronized with everyone else's; in World War I, the hideous slaughter of Allied soldiers at Gallipoli resulted from the watches of two commanders—one governing the artillery barrage, the other the infantry charge—stubbornly refusing to tell the same time.

Time comes in several flavors: *Solar time* is measured from one midday to the next—the "solar day." *Sidereal time* is reckoned not by the sun but by the stars (Latin *sōl, sōlis* means 'sun' and *sīdus, sīderis* means 'star'); since each day the earth has traveled another 1/365th of the way around its orbit, the sidereal day—the duration between consecutive risings of a star—is about four minutes shorter than the solar one.

Although Ben Franklin, while serving as America's ambassador to the court of the hapless Louis XVI and Marie Antoinette, had suggested setting all the clocks an hour earlier or later depending on the time of year, daylight saving time was not adopted until the 1940s, and then it functioned primarily as a wartime measure to conserve energy. Daylight saving time shifts midday to about 1:00 P.M. for the summer months. Standard time is whatever isn't daylight saving time, i.e., when midday is more or less at noon.

Is time truly continuous? Ed Fredkin, who believes the cosmos is a computer, has proposed a thought experiment: Suppose the cosmos was actually ticking along in discrete chunks of activity, with gaps of inactivity in between. The ticks can be very small, of course; the frequency of a cesium-beam resonator is over nine billion a second. (Cesium-regulated quartz-crystal clocks are the most accurate ones made so far; the quartz crystal in your digital wristwatch vibrates a mere few hundred thousand times a second.) Fredkin's suggestion was that if the universe really were a tick-tock affair, we wouldn't know it, because we would be tick-tocking along with it, so we would perceive time as a continuous flow. Or as Borbonius, a poetaster of the second century A.D. put it, *"Tempora mutantur, nōs et mutāmur cum illīs"* ('Times change, and we change with them').

"Time," said a north country sage, "is nature's way of keeping everything from happening at once." Our scientific minds follow Newton, who, eager to quantify everything, defined time as duration. But we all experience time subjectively, and our sense of time changes with advancing age, as Piaget and others studying perception of time in children have shown. We have "internal clocks," both biological and psychological. (Who of us, having set the alarm unusually early, has not awakened a half hour before it?) Yet when asked to estimate elapsed time under a minute, we typically overestimate small fractions of a second, but underestimate more than a half-second—and the degree of error is affected by whether we do this in silence or with some background noise.

The internal rhythms of our bodies are on several different periods. The cycle people are most aware of is the *circadian* (literally, 'around a day'—closer to twenty-five hours, left to its own devices, but daily yanked back into sync with the earth's twenty-four-hour rotation— what alarm clocks are for). Other cycles are evident in some metabolic functions. Human cell division dances to an *ultradian* ('beyond a day'—occurring more than once a day) rhythm: There are certain times of day when our cells multiply, and others when they don't.

Cancerous cells, as part of their internal disruption and confusion, fail to obey this timetable, replicating out of control throughout the day. Various cancer drugs block cell replication indiscriminately, preventing all cells from multiplying, including the healthy ones. However, when chemotherapy treatments are synchronized with the body's normal nonreplicating hours, the drug blocks the replication of malignant cells only.

Next to the daily cycle, the lunar month seems most with us: The tides are tied to it as is the human menstrual cycle—the English words *tide* and *time* come from a common Indo-European root (**deH-*), meaning something like 'divide,' while *menstrual* comes via the Latin word for 'month'—*mēnsis*—from the Indo-European root **meH-*, 'measure' that underlies the words *metric, month,* the *-meal* of *piecemeal,* and *measure* itself. Another cycle is that of approximately a week: the *circaseptan* (literally, 'around seven') rhythm. The week has always puzzled scholars of time because it has no clear connection to the rest of the cosmos: It's not even a quarter of a lunar month, which is twenty-nine-plus days.

As an internal natural rhythm, the circaseptan is a faint blip; computer analysis is required to tease its effects out from surrounding "noise" in the data. But it's there, all right: Quasi-weekly cycles show up in our body temperature, our blood acidity, the amount of calcium excreted in our urine, and in the level of our cortisol, the so-called "coping" hormone. It is no accident that the crisis in pneumonia usually comes on the seventh day. Some normally dormant mechanisms of the body's defense systems apparently operate on a circaseptan rhythm once they have been triggered by an invading pathogen. Kidney transplant patients tend to reject the alien organ seven, fourteen, twenty-one, or twenty-eight days after the operation. Subconsciously, we keep track of the time.

But what of our conscious perceptions of time? These may be very subjective, yet they still work. We carry around in our minds a rough idea of how big things are and how long they last; time, like length, volume, and weight, has its own familiar folk metrics. In everyday life, "down the road about two football fields," "bigger than a bread box," "a lump of butter the size of an egg," and "two Hail Marys" quantify by exemplary mental image; we do not feel the need to get out the tape measure or the stopwatch.

"How far is it from Albany to Boston?" By car? Three hours, perhaps. But in the train club car, a reasonable answer might be "Six pints [of beer]." How long did Rosemary Wood have her foot on the erase pedal for the Nixon tapes? "About an Alice"—i.e., the length of time it takes Arlo Guthrie to sing "Alice's Restaurant," around eighteen minutes.

In Sweden at the turn of this century, the *Pusthall* ('bout of work') was the usual measure of time between breaks on the farm; it ran to about an hour and a half, give or take. Then clocks came to the countryside, along with the farmhouse "gruel bell," rung to divide up the day of the workers in the fields. This gave rise to a number of satirical songs about hard hours and bad food—precursors of Bob Dylan's "Ain't Gonna Work on Maggie's Farm No More"—with refrains that imitate the gruel-bell's ringing.

What the Swedish agricultural workers went through was in part a shift from task time to clock time. Every time we try to finish a job on time and don't, we feel pulled in two directions by the task that is still to be finished and the clock that has run out. ("I was on schedule, but the deadline came too early.") The souls in Dante's *Purgatorio* worked out their penance until they were purged, whereupon they realized, through divine enlightenment, that their job was done and got to move one level up. This is the epitome of task time, as opposed to clock time: hashmarks on a prisoner's cell wall; clock-watching by bored pupils (and their teachers) yearning for a break.

The *break* interrupts subjective time; it is the stoppering of the psychological water clock. Time off doesn't count. (There may, of course, be rules built into the system limiting the break; otherwise, Denver could use one of its time-outs to block the Buffalo field goal attempt for, say, a whole season.) Sacred time in some cultures is divorced from "real" (secular, workaday) time by rituals involving, as Edmund Leach put it, "funny hats and false noses": for example, the Mummers' Day parade in Philadelphia on the first day of the new year, or Mardi Gras in New Orleans to kick off the penitential season of Lent. In embracing the human seven-day cycle, early Christians transferred the Jewish custom of not working on the Sabbath to the first day of the week; thanks to the Puritans, Yankee blue laws made sure, until very recently, that everybody knew Sunday's time was not for business as usual.

Breaking is, of course, one way of dividing—usually, rather abruptly. We speak of the *break of billiard balls* when the cue ball first strikes the racked triangle, or of a *break in the ice floe* (great if you're on a trapped ship, not so good if you're traveling by dogsled), or a *break in the weather*. "*Gimme a break!*" says the felon caught red-handed—i.e., let me off easier than I should expect if the system rattled along its inexorable way. "I'll give you a break on the price," says the jeweler confidentially. *Break points* in a computer program are instructions causing the execution of the program to pause, or be paused, at various strategic locations in the code in order to see how things are going, this being a standard way of debugging. The line between *break* and *pause* is often blurred; but on the IBM Enhanced Keyboard, a neat distinction is shown on the BREAK/PAUSE key that, depending on whether or not you depress the CTRL key at the same time, either suspends operation of your program until you are ready to resume it, or else tells the program that it's time to stop for good.

SIX

"SIX OF ONE AND a half dozen of the other," we say—a distinction without a difference. But things can be the same in different ways. We take for granted numerical equations, as in "$2 + 4 = 6$," and, if prodded, geometric congruence, as in "these two triangles are congruent because the corresponding sides in each are the same length"—this is sometimes called *Euclidean congruence,* after, no surprise, the geometer Euclid—not to be confused with *similarity:* "These two triangles are similar because the corresponding angles in each are the same, but they can still be of two different sizes."

There is *transposition,* as in music: "Let's try playing it in E flat instead." (But is it still the "same" tune if you take it a whole tone up, or down a major third? Or put it into a minor key? Or play it backwards at half tempo?) Then there's *metathesis,* another kind of transposition: "Put *A* where *B* is, and vice versa"—as when we write "Protland, ME" or Dr. Spooner referred to his sovereign, Victoria, as the "queer old Dean."

Another kind of sameness: Transformational grammarians speak of sentences with different *surface structures* that share a common *deep structure.* For example, "My brother wrote this sentence" and "This sentence was written by my brother" may both be derived from the same underlying semantic representation, i.e., at some level, they *mean* the same thing. Or consider the phenomenon of *translation,* which may aspire to the exact replication in one language of that which is said in another but often falls far short of that goal: *"Traduttore, traditore"* ('translator = traitor') is an old Italian barb—and an example of another kind of equivalence, the pun.

Puns, which play on similar sounds coupled to dissimilar senses, are often called the lowest form of humor; certainly they are the most maligned form of wordplay. We emit deep groans when they appear as the punch lines of outrageous shaggy-dog stories: What happened when Larry Lobster played hooky from the heavenly choir to visit his old bivalve buddy, now bandmaster at the dance hall in Hell ("I lost my harp in Sam Clam's disco").

Yet puns, as Walter Redfern points out in his *Puns*, "illuminate the nature of language in general." It is no accident that we pun furiously in our sleep, nor that phonetic free association can give us the same kind of pleasure daydreams do. Freud was quick to seize upon punning as a mechanism for coping with ambivalence, akin to using words that carry double and opposite meanings (such as *cleave:* My tongue cleaves to the roof of my mouth; I cleave the billet with a hatchet), and to certain slips of the tongue.

To pun is at once to make something new in words while broadening the semantic content of existing ones; punning equates things we had thought unrelated. Punsters subvert language, making it jump through hoops. "Pleased to indulge in the ingenious technique without worrying about the preposterous conclusions," grumbled one critic of both Lewis Carroll and the Sophists. Maybe so, but writers from Heraclitus to Chesterton have tickled generations of readers with the ability to tolerate ambiguity and verbal sleight of hand.

The hoops at the punster's disposal are chiefly auditory: The hymn verse that begins "Lead on, O Kinky Turtle," the revolutionary tracts hidden under the towels in the *Lenin closet,* and the forgotten nighttime dose of the male fertility drug, or, *nocturnal omission,* all turn on what linguists call *minimal pairs*—words or phrases whose pronunciation differs slightly but significantly. The shortest man in the Bible (*Bildad the Shoe-height*) and the cattle ranch named *Focus* by its owners' mother (because that's where the *sons raise meat*) rely on *homophones*—words with identical pronunciations but different meanings.

There are orthographic hoops as well: *homographs* (the homophones' orthographic opposite number) allow the possibility of glossing *unionized gases* as 'candidates for office in the AFL-CIO (or Writers' Guild).' And, farther out into left field are *anagrams,* where the same letters are used but switched around. So François Rabelais gave himself the pseudonym *Alcofribar Nasier;* the town with America's widest Main Street, Keene, NH, is an anagram of *hen knee;* and one episode of the BBC's "Fawlty Towers" series showed the hotel's sign with its letters rearranged to spell *flowery twats.* The *antigram* goes this one better yet, by reshuffling a name into its opposite: *The Louvre* becomes *True Hovel,* and *The Waldorf, Dwarf Hotel.*

The virtuoso punster does not hesitate, when the appropriate (or inappropriate) opportunity presents itself, to mix and match these types. Consider, for example, Sir John Harington's scurrilous pun, "Pope Sisesinke," on the name of Pope Sixtus V, who reaffirmed the excommunication of Harington's patron, Queen Elizabeth I, *sink* here meaning 'cesspool,' but the play on words turning both on the pope's name (which translates literally as 'Sixth the fifth') and on the Middle English expression, *to set on sink and sice,* i.e., 'to bet on a five and a six' (compare French *cinq* 'five' and *six* 'six'), or, 'to wager on long odds,' the likelihood of rolling a five and a six with two dice being, however desirable, disfavored by the laws of probability—Harington's point being, presumably, that Sixtus V was both rash and, well, smelly.

Somewhere along the way from Middle English to Modern English, *to set on sink and sice* got transformed into *to be at sixes and sevens,* presumably on something like the idea that more is better: If *x* is good, then $(x + 1)$ must be even spiffier. This has its contemporary analogy: A commercial product (*Our Product*) often gives way to a later version marketed under the name of "*Our Product +* "—Sprint Plus, the long-distance service; Mac Plus, Apple's successor to its early Macintosh; Fifty Plus, a bank account that cleverly combines the suggestion of more and better service with its availability only to those over a half-century old. A cynic might argue that, from a marketing point of view, these pluses are essentially hyperbolic, designed to give an illusion of added value merely to counteract the inevitable drop-off in the sales curve of any prod-

uct's life cycle. If so, Bjarne Stroustrup, the progenitor of the programming language C + +, implied that his was a better version of
the language C by two degrees, in the bargain punning on " + + "—
the standard sign in C meaning "increment this."

But what does it mean to say that rolling a six and a seven is
even better than rolling a five and a six, since it is not in fact
possible to roll both a six and a seven (i.e., thirteen) in a single
throw of two dice? Bumping *sink and sice* up to *six(es) and sev-
en(s)* would seem to push the normal laws of chance beyond their
limit. Well, all we can say with certainty is that of the two metaphors, the more extravagant one was a keeper, while the more
modest five-and-six got its gold watch, English apparently feeling
no poorer for getting along on just one word for 'five' as, a small
number of compounds excepted (e.g., *cinquefoil*), *sink* sank into
utter obscurity, as did *sice*.

The replacement of *set on sink and sice* by *be at sixes and sevens* eventually entailed a change of underlying meaning in addition
to the change in surface structure—from 'wager on long odds' to
'be in a state of disorder or disarray.' Same thing, only different,
we might say, indulging our taste for vernacular oxymoron while
evading the question of whether we're talking about a distinction
without a difference or a difference without a distinction—or, as
Paul Klee described the task of the artist, "making the equivalent
equal."

For what it is worth, the original Indo-Europeans seem to have had
no standard word for *equal:* There are no obvious cognates in other
Indo-European languages for Latin *aequus,* the source of English
equal, equality, equity, and the *equi-* of *equivalent, equilateral,* and
equinox (but not of *equitation,* which is from *equus* 'horse,' which
reminds us of the hoary joke about the little town the travel brochure
called "unique." A disgruntled tourist who'd been there reported
that it was "unique" only if one chose to derive the word from *unus
equus*—'one horse'). *Aequus* originally meant 'level, flat, even,'
hence 'on the same horizontal plane with' (as the two pans of a
balance scale). From this it was a short hop to 'evenly balanced;
equal in distance, height, quantity, etc.,' then 'matching, equal,

alike,' and finally 'fair, just.' (Compare English *Level with me* and *Don't get mad, get even*.) *Even*—'flat, level, equal, equally balanced' (as in *on an even keel*)—has cognates in the Germanic languages but nowhere else; its numerical sense of 'divisible by 2' is a very late afterthought.

The term that the Romans used for 'equal (in number, intensity, magnitude, or other measurable quality)' is *pār*. Here again, a search for Indo-European cognates is in vain: *Pār*, like *aequus*, seems to have sprung up in the soil of Italy all of its own accord; it's tempting to try to relate it to Greek *para-*, 'alongside,' (as in *parallel*) but it won't wash. But although *pār* is an orphan, it does not lack for descendants: including French (and English) *pair*, and—from the sense of Charlemagne's *douze pairs* (the twelve equal knights)—English *peer*, as in *House of Peers* and *jury of one's peers*. Nor may we omit *pari-mutuel*, a fair and square steal from French *pari mutuel* 'shared betting': the *pari* part is our Latin friend *pār* again, here in the sense that if I bet *x* amount, you'll match it; and the *mutuel* suggests that "you" may be plural, and you'll all share the gain or loss equally, or at least proportionally to the amount you put in (minus, heh heh, the cut due to the house). This model, without which today's horse-racing industry could not exist, also made possible the financing of the Hanseatic League, and was thus as important to the rise of business as usual in the Western world as was the accounting equation of double-entry bookkeeping (Assets = Liabilities + Equity).

Same comes from an Indo-European root (**sem-*) meaning 'one,' the same one that underlies Greek *homo-* (as in *homogenized*), Latin *simul* 'at the same time,' whence came *simultaneous* and the *sin-* of English *single*. The Greek word for 'same'—again, of unknown origin—is *isos*, which appears in such English borrowings as *isosceles* (the kind of triangle that has two sides—*skeloi* are literally 'legs'—of equal length), *isobar*, and *isogloss*, the latter both being lines on a map: The *isobar* connects areas of equal atmospheric pressure; an *isogloss* marks the border between two populations of speakers of a language according to how they say something (e.g., where a *sub* becomes a *hoagie* or an *Italian* or a *grinder* or a *hero*). Alas, **isornith* (*iso-* + *ornithos* 'bird')—the border of the colored patches on the maps in bird books that show habitat limits for each species—has gone unattested till now.

Of the symbols denoting sameness, the most familiar is the equal sign (=), generally credited to Robert Recorde's 1557 treatise on algebra, *The Whetstone of Witte*. "No two things could be more equal (than two parallel lines)," he argued; and his equal sign won out in the end, despite grumbling by Continental mathematicians who had been getting along fine with an em dash.

In some computer programming languages, the meaning of the equal sign varies with context. For example, the following BASIC program fragment employs the equal sign twice, first in a comparison and then in an assignment:

IF RATING = "Good_Employee" THEN SALARY = 50000

In other words, if the employee's RATING is equal to "Good_Employee," then make the employee's SALARY equal to 50000.

In programming languages, using the same symbol for different meanings is called *overloading:* Unlike BASIC, the languages Pascal and C, while they have nothing against overloading in principle, in practice distinguish between comparison expressions and assignment statements. Pascal uses an equal sign (=) by itself for comparison and colon, equal sign (: =) for assignment. In C, assignment statements get a single equal sign (=) and comparison expressions a double one (= =). Thus, the Pascal and C translations of the BASIC code fragment that assigns good employees salaries of fifty thousand dollars would be, respectively:

IF RATING = "Good_Employee"
    THEN SALARY : = 50000;

and

if (RATING = = 'Good_Employee')
    SALARY = 50000;

In spoken languages, it's the same thing, only different. That is, spoken languages allow for a certain amount of overloading while offering a variety of means for resolving (or, in the case of punning, exploiting) the potential ambiguity inherent in letting one thing stand for more than one other thing: context (both grammatical and semantic), orthography, and such socio-linguistic cues as tone of voice or facial expression can all come into play to ensure that the intended mapping takes place between what the followers of the linguist Ferdinand de Saussure termed the *signifiant* ('that which means something') and the *signifié* ('that which is meant').

This sort of mapping has a number of analogs in the world of mathematics. For example, suppose you have a bunch of people and a bunch of bicycles, and you want to determine if there are enough bicycles to go around (that is, you want to map people to bicycles or bicycles to people): Method Number One: Count the people, count the bicycles, and compare the numbers. Method Number Two: Tell everybody to get on a bicycle and ride across the street, then see if there are any bikes or pedestrians left over.

Another way of putting this is that the bicycles constitute one set and the people another. The sets are the same size if and only if each person has exactly one bike and each bike is in the hands of exactly one person (that is, there is a one-to-one mapping of people to bicycles and bicycles to people).

Ticket sales for what is now called "festival seating" and used to be called "general admission" use the first method: Promoters count the seats and print that many tickets, knowing that when the tickets run out so will the seating. This has its dangerous side: When the gates opened for a concert given a decade ago by The Who in Cincinnati, Ohio, people were trampled, some fatally, in the scramble for the good seats. (As a result of this and other catastrophes, promoters shy away from festival seating these days.)

The advantage of the second method—which works better for matching bicycles with riders than for matching concert-goers with available seating (the event at Woodstock in 1969 being, perhaps, an exception to this rule of thumb)—is that you can compare the sets even if you don't know how many members are in either, thereby saving yourself the trouble of counting the members of each set being compared since the two sets cancel each other out.

Like musical chairs, the one-bike-one-rider problem can be understood using what mathematicians call the *pigeonhole principle*. If you try to fit too many pigeons into too few holes, some of the pigeons are going to have to move over in their holes to make room for a second pigeon. Or some passenger will have to give up a booked seat on an overbooked flight. Or somebody without a dance partner has to waltz with a Windsor chair.

By the pigeonhole principle it can be shown that there are people in New York City with exactly the same number of hairs on their heads. Let us suppose that even the hairiest person in New York has no more than 1,000,000 hairs. Now imagine 1,000,001 boxes, numbered 0 through 1,000,000. Into each box we'll drop a slip of paper with the name of a New Yorker having the number of hairs indicated on the box. (Box 0 will contain the names of all the completely bald people.) When we're done, we'll have distributed 8 million names among 1,000,001 boxes, so clearly at least one box has more than one name in it, and those names correspond to people with the same number of hairs.

Note that the pigeonhole principle does not tell you in advance which people have the same number of hairs on their head, only that there are some with the same number. Nor does it tell you what that number might be. This should seem magical rather than suspicious—you know a general truth without knowing the specifics. With the bikes and cyclists, it's the same thing (only different). You know nothing about either individual set, but you know that each is the same size as the other. You *could* count each set and compare, but it's easier to pair them up and look at the spillover.

The set-theoretical notion of "sets the same size" has its counterpart in the poetic figure *metonymy,* as in "All hands on deck!" or "Let's do a head count." We can talk about *head* count when we mean *people* count because we can map either set onto the other, one to one: Barring abnormal circumstances like Robespierre's Reign of Terror, we know that every head is attached to one body and vice versa. (The mapping of hands to people is somewhat less straight-forward; witness the case of Captain Hook.)

A quick side trip to the land of syllogism, which has more to do with set theory than first meets the eye . . . The first type of syllogism, to which the medieval Scholastics assigned the mnemonic *Barbara*, goes like this:

> All human beings are mortal.
> Socrates is human.
> Therefore, Socrates is mortal.

Another way of putting this is:

> The set "humans" is a subset of the set of mortal beings.
> Socrates is a member of the set of human beings.
> Therefore, Socrates is also a member of the set of mortals.

We can represent this in a Venn diagram (named for the British mathematician, John Venn, born in 1834).

Figure 11: Humans, Mortals, and Others

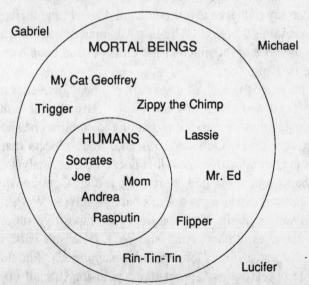

We've also put some beings outside the domain of MORTAL BE-INGS—one fallen angel and two in good standing—to indicate that they are not members of the class of mortal beings; we'll get back to them shortly.

A statement such as "All men are mortal" is called a *universal affirmative*, because it makes an assertion about all members of a class or set. In this form it is called the *positive*.

The *contrapositive* of "All *A* are *B*" is "All *not-B* are *not-A*." (Strictly speaking, "All *not-B* are *not-A*" is the full *contrapositive* of the proposition "All *A* are *B*," of which the *partial contrapositive* is "All *not-A* are *not-B*.") If the positive is true, so is the full contrapositive. "No immortal is human" follows directly and inevitably from "All humans are mortal," and vice versa. From the diagram it is clear that as the set of humans falls entirely within the set of mortal beings, nothing outside that larger set (i.e., the immortals) can be a part of the smaller set either. Thus, a proposition and its (full) contrapositive may be said to be *equipollent*, literally, 'having equal strength'.

Can the positive be otherwise converted? Well, the *inverse* of "All *A* are *B*" ("No *A* is not *B*")—"No human is immortal"—is true enough, but the *converse* ("All *B* are *A*") is not necessarily so. The best we can say in that case is this: "If all *A* are *B* (and there are some *A*), at least some *B* are *A*." The last Albanian monarch is dead; but only one member of the much larger class of dead people answers to the name of King Zog.

Take the proposition "All dogs bark." The equivalent contrapositive is "If it doesn't bark, it's not a dog." Because these things are logically equivalent, observations tending to confirm one should tend to confirm the other. Outside, I run into three objects that tend to confirm the contrapositive: a cat that doesn't bark (Analysis: Well, it doesn't bark, and sure enough, it's not a dog. Contrapositive supported); a postal carrier who doesn't bark (Analysis: Well, it doesn't bark, and sure enough, it's not a dog. Contrapositive supported); a mailbox that doesn't bark (Analysis: Well, it doesn't bark, and sure enough, it's not a dog. Contrapositive supported). Should any of these three observations support the conclusion that all dogs bark?

This problem has vexed philosophers of science for years, and much has been said about it elsewhere; we're not going to solve it here.

Which is not to say that we will let sleeping dogs lie: The fact that logical equivalence and practical equivalence are not identical nips at our heels. Set theorists are unperturbed by this. Indeed, modern set theory, first developed by Georg Cantor (1845–1918), accommodates the notion of multiple, independent forms of equivalence, using the notion of *relations* to do so. In set theory, a (*binary*) *relation* is a set of ordered pairs whose individual items are culled from another set. A relation is said to exist *over a set*. The relation catalogs which individual elements in the set are related to each other.

For example, among the authors of this book, Alex Humez is eldest, Nick Humez is next oldest, and Joe Maguire is youngest. We can speak of the *Is older than* relation over the set of *Authors of this book:* Alex is older than Nick. Nick is older than Joe. Alex is older than Joe.

The relation has three elements; each is an ordered pair whose first item is someone older than its second (e.g., {Alex, Nick}). This relation has a noteworthy characteristic: It is *transitive*. Because Alex is older than Nick and Nick is older than Joe, Alex must be older than Joe.

Over the same set, we can create another relation, called *Has the same surname as*. Alex has the same surname as Nick. Nick has the same surname as Alex. Alex has the same surname as Alex. Nick has the same surname as Nick. Joe has the same surname as Joe.

This relation is *symmetric;* Alex has the same surname as Nick, therefore Nick has the same surname as Alex.

The relation is also *reflexive,* because we can say things like ''Joe has the same surname as Joe.'' A relation that's not reflexive: *Is the brother of*. Alex is the brother of Nick. Nick is the brother of Alex.

This relation is not reflexive because none of us is his own brother.

If a relation happens to be symmetric, transitive, and reflexive, it is called an *equivalence relation*. And a set can typically have many different equivalence relations. The set of human beings has *Has the same zodiacal sign as* and *Has the same number of teeth as,* both perfectly good equivalence relations. Astrology is not equivalent to dental hygiene, however. Just because one Sagittarius is toothless doesn't mean they all are.

This is why the typical set theorist is not disturbed that "All dogs bark" is easier to confirm than its logically equivalent contrapositive. Logical equivalence is not identical to practical equivalence, and there is no reason to expect otherwise. What's equivalent on one scale might not be equivalent on another. Or as George Orwell would say, "Some animals are more equal than others." (The most common equivalence relation by the way, is *equality* itself. It is transitive, symmetric, and reflexive.)

Every equivalence relation over a set has an equivalent *partition* of the set. Any set can be *partitioned*—that is, split into nonoverlapping subsets. The natural numbers can be sorted exhaustively into odds and evens. The people of New York City can be divided into bald people and those whose heads have one or more hairs. Or, as seen above, you can further subdivide them into those with no hair, those with one hair, those with two, and so on.

Bona fide subsets of this sort must be (1) nonoverlapping: A man who has a certain number of hairs on his head has only that number, and no other. (He may share that number with other people or he may be the only New Yorker with that number—he may even decide to grow a beard and move to San Francisco—but neither case poses a problem.) They must also be (2) exhaustive: Each element in the original set ends up in one of the subsets, with no leftovers. (Mortals are either alive or dead; you are born under exactly one sign; an integer is either odd or even.)

Oddness, applied to numbers, is not debatable although we've heard it said that 2, as the only prime that's even, is the oddest number of all. Oddness and evenness are a special case of an entire grab bag of equivalence relations (or partitions, if you prefer) found in modular arithmetic, dreamed up by Johann Carl Friedrich Gauss (1777–1855). According to Gauss, two integers x and y are congruent modulo n if x/n yields the same integer remainder as y/n.

To take an example from the seven-day-a-week calendar, part of everyday life: The day after Tuesday is Wednesday. Modular arithmetic tells us that twenty-nine days from Tuesday will also be a

Wednesday. How so? The numerical players here are seven (the number of days from one Tuesday to the next) and one (the number of days from any Tuesday to the following Wednesday). If today is Tuesday, any multiple of seven days from now (0, 7, 14, 21, 28, . . .) is also going to be a Tuesday. The modular arithmetic way of expressing this is (*multiple of 7*) *mod 7 is congruent to 0,* which is to say that when you divide a multiple of seven by seven you get a remainder of zero. What about Wednesdays? If Wednesday is one day "more than" Tuesday, then if today is still Tuesday and if the number of days from today is one more than a multiple of seven (1, 8, 15, 22, 29, . . .), then that day will be a Wednesday. The modular arithmetic way of expressing this is ((*multiple of 7*) *plus 1*) *mod 7 is congruent to 1*, which is to say that when you divide one more than a multiple of seven by seven, you get a whole-number (integer) remainder of one. All of which is to say that we can say 1 is congruent (modulo 7) to 29 without embarrassment or fear of contradiction:

$$29(mod\ 7) = 1$$

Not surprisingly, notions of equality and equivalence turn up in plenty of political and social systems: a chicken in every pot; one man, one vote; and so on. Even less surprising is that further inspection of the fair-minded political rallying cries reveals potential inequities. A chicken in every pot, but can some pots have several chickens? (Remember the pigeonhole principle?)

One person, one vote is also less fair than it seems. As a model for equitable distribution of power in a democracy, it has some deficiencies, letting an unpopular candidate win by dividing votes among several of his or her more popular opponents. Approval voting is a fairer alternative, letting each voter approve or disapprove of each candidate. One person, one vote unfairly favors those with strong preferences for a single candidate and penalizes those whose preferences are more subtle, or who have strong distaste for a particular candidate. Approval voting eliminates this inequity, but meets resistance in some quarters as undemocratic.

On the individual scale, this can be carried too far, of course: A certain Maine farmer, having heard a lecture on socialism at the Lyceum, was trying to convert his neighbor, explaining how under such a system everything would be share and share alike. "You mean, if you had two barns, you'd give me one?" asked his neighbor, skeptically. "Yes, Enoch, I would," the new proselyte said. "And if you had two cows, you'd give me one?" "Yes, Enoch, if I had two cows, I'd give you one." "And if you had two hogs . . . ?" "Damn you, Enoch, you *know* I've got two hogs!"

SEVEN

EVERYBODY LIKES THE number seven: To an even greater extent than thirteen, it has a mystique that cuts across culture and time. It's the smallest integer that won't divide 360 evenly and the largest prime below ten. Psychologically, seven seems to be the largest number of objects or separate colors that the human mind can readily keep track of when newly exposed to them. In the biblical book of Deuteronomy, "seven" is synonymous with "many." Seven is one more fingers than even a "normal" polydactyl human has; the Irish hero Cuchulain was said to have had seven fingers on each hand.

In China, odd numbers were characterized by *yang*, the male principle. Despite this, seven is thought to have something of the *yin* (the female principle) about it because of its association with women: A baby girl gets her first teeth at seven months, loses them at seven years, begins menstruating at twice seven (fourteen), stops menstruating at seven times seven (forty-nine). Men, on the other hand, are supposed to live according to multiples of eight. In both China and Tibet, mourning for the dead takes forty-nine days, with ceremonies and sacrifices marking the seven stages of seven days during which the soul gradually severs itself from this world and makes its way to the next life.

In Japanese folklore, there are seven gods of luck: *Benten,* goddess of love; *Bishamon,* god of war; *Daikoku,* god of wealth; *Ebisu,* god of self-effacement; *Hotei,* god of good humor; and the two gods of longevity, *Fukurokuji* and *Jojorin.* Hindu tradition honors the Seven Rishis, the semidivine sages through whom the Vedas were transmitted to humanity; they made the dawn break and the sun rise with their hymns, and when they died they became the seven stars of the Big Dipper, and their wives became the Pleiades. And in Egypt, seven seems to have supplanted four as an earlier favorite: The dead got an audience with seven gods and seven snakes, being met in the other world by seven cows and a bull (recalling Joseph's dream of the seven fat and seven lean cows by which he foretold the fat and famine years to Pharaoh), and the correct dosage for medicine was seven pills.

The Greeks associated the number seven with Apollo, whose feast days always fell on the seventh of the month. There were seven Hesperides, the daughters of the west wind to whom Heracles went to fetch the golden apples. (Their fabled islands beyond Gibraltar have been identified with the Canaries.) Thebes had seven gates. When Eteocles set up shop as tyrant after Oedipus died, and his brother Polynices marched against him, seven pairs of champions fought to the death for a gate apiece. Niobe had seven sons and seven daughters; the lyre had seven strings. And it was the Greek philosopher Philo who observed that twenty-eight, the approximate number of days in the lunar month, is the sum of all the positive integers from 1 through 7.

The Judeo-Christian fancy for the number seven is rich in examples, possibly dating back from before Abraham: The Chaldeans were known to repeat incantations seven times, to bake seven loaves for sacrifices, to tie seven knots in sacred cords. There were thought to be seven directions (later supplanted by four), and seven bright heavenly bodies (the sun, the moon, and the visible planets). It seems likely that assigning one of these to each day gave rise to the seven-day week (rather than its being a quarter of a lunar month, a sloppy fit at best). Whatever the case, Mesopotamia knew a good period between holidays when it saw one; it seems very likely that the Jews were celebrating Sabbath every seven days long before anybody wrote down Genesis to explain why.

In Hebrew, 'to swear' literally means 'to come under the influence of seven things'—e.g., there were seven lambs given at the swearing of the oath between Abraham and Abimelech. When Joshua fought the battle of Jericho, his army processed around the city on each of seven days, on the last day doing so seven times accompanied by seven priests blowing on rams' horns, the general ruckus causing the walls of the city to come tumbling down. Delilah wormed Samson's secret out of him on the seventh day of their wedding feast, whereupon he was shorn of seven locks of hair and bound with seven withy cords; but when his hair grew back, he could not be restrained, even by an unspecified number of bronze fetters.

Seven days are allotted to the feasts of Passover (*Pesach,* whence came, via Latin, English *paschal,* 'having to do with Easter') and Tabernacles (*Sukkoth*). The High Holidays—the Jewish New Year (*Rosh Hashanah*), and the Day of Atonement (*Yom Kippur*)—fall in what is actually the seventh month of the Jewish calendar. Exodus dictates seven days for the ordination of priests and the consecration of altars; seven days was also the period required for purification from the worst kinds of ritual defilement.

Christianity added a wealth of sevens of its own. There are seven petitions in the Lord's Prayer, seven parables in the New Testament book of Matthew, seven sorrows of Mary, seven last words of Christ from the Cross (though there is substantial disagreement as to what those words were and whether there were *really* seven of them—*The New Catholic Encyclopedia* lists, appropriately enough, seven different versions of the Seven Words from the Cross, observing that "The number seven is accidental," i.e., whichever reporting of Christ's last words one takes as gospel, the number of words doesn't work out to seven), and the subsequent appearance of the resurrected Christ to seven of His disciples. Revelations abounds with references to the number seven. And the Epistles list seven afflictions, seven gifts, seven qualities of heavenly wisdom, and seven virtues that supplement faith; the Middle Ages would list faith itself as one of the seven Virtues, the others being hope and charity—these three are mentioned in the famous passage from Paul's first letter to the Corinthians—plus what are also called the Four Cardinal Virtues: justice, prudence, temperance and fortitude.

In the first act of *King Lear,* when Goneril has just sent half of her father's retinue packing, Lear's Fool tries to coax him out of his high dudgeon with the old Pleiades teaser: "The reason why the Seven Stars are no more than seven is a pretty reason." Lear gets it in one. "Because they are not eight?" "Yes indeed," answers the jester: "Thou wouldst make a good fool."

Actually, they were both wrong. Nowadays, the naked eye can only see six stars, represented in the logo on the front of every Subaru automobile—*Subaru* is the Japanese name for the Pleiades. A seventh star—Pleione—is a star of variable magnitude, which is to say that its brightness increases and diminishes on the regular cycle of its nuclear furnace, making it more or less visible. At present, it can't be seen with the naked eye. Actually, the Pleiades cluster, in the constellation of Taurus, contains hundreds of stars. The seven visible to the Greco-Roman world were said to be the daughters of Atlas the Titan—Maia, Electra, Celaeno, Taygeta, Merope, Alcyone, and Asterope—turned into stars and set in the heavens. The Babylonians, on the other hand, considered the Pleiades to be the personification of the seven weapons that Irra sent against the world, images of which were buried at house gates as good-luck talismans.

In most societies, the heavens are the abode of gods and heroes from mythic times; but Heaven, as the place that you get to go when you die if you've been good, is not always in the sky. The early Irish believed in a spirit world contiguous to this one at all points, but normally inaccessible to mortals except at death. One of Finn McCool's heroic attributes was that by thrusting his thumb under his "Tooth of Mystic Knowledge," he would go into a trance in which he journeyed into and out of the other world painlessly—in stark contrast to the banshees (Irish Gaelic *bean sídhe,* 'woman of the fairies'), sent to this world to fetch the souls of the dead back with them, who express their discomfort with the howls called *keening* (*caoine,* 'lamentation').

The Greeks believed that the souls of the virtuous went to the Elysian Fields, while the wicked went to Tartarus, where spectacularly bad things happened to them: Tantalus's perpetual thirst and hunger, Sisyphus's rock, Ixion's wheel. Everybody else either wandered around forever in Hades not doing anything in particular (except when epic heroes like Odysseus and Aeneas got to drop in for a chat) or else got reborn, first drinking water from the river Lethe to forget their past lives.

The Greek word for 'soul' is *pneuma,* which also means 'wind' and 'breath'—*pneumonia* is a disease that does a number on the equipment that you use for breathing; *pneu* is the French word for bicycle or automobile tire (or tyre, if you prefer), something with air in it. Latin *spīritus* means 'breath' as well as 'soul, spirit' (the latter sense being the one in *Spīritus Sanctus* 'Holy Ghost'). Today we say "Where there's life, there's hope," while the Romans said *Dum spīrō, spērō,* literally 'While I breathe, I hope.' Both the Greeks and the Romans figured that once somebody wasn't breathing anymore, the soul left with the breath, from which it was a short step to believing that the breath and soul were one. The other standard Latin word for 'soul,' *anima,* also meant 'air,' and it is from this latter sense that we get the terms *animal* (i.e., a breathing organism) and *animated* ('lively' or, as we might say, 'spirited').

Ancient Jewish ideas of an afterlife were limited to *sheol,* a dark, nondescript place of departed spirits, and *gehenna,* a sort of hell. The name is derived from *ge Hinnom,* 'Valley of Hinnom,' where the Canaanites had offered human sacrifices, and, later, where Jerusalem maintained its common dump—a barren, foul place where ground fires now and then ignited of their own accord. Nobody got to go to Heaven as such.

For its notions of the afterlife and where one would get to spend it, win, lose, or (as a later refinement in church dogma) draw, the early Christians turned instead to the Hellenic model, with its clear division between the good guys and the bad guys. As its name implies—the underlying root seems to have meant 'cover, conceal, stash away'—*Hell* was established down below, a sentiment few miners would have contradicted. The torments of the Christian Hell were freely borrowed from the Greeks: Some medieval scholars even considered Tartarus, including its mythic inmates, to be a wholly owned subsidiary of Hell.

Paradise was the Greek translation of an Avestan (Old Persian) word for a walled hunting park of the sort maintained throughout the Persian empire for its noble class (*paradeisos* meant 'walled around'). As such, the Garden of Eden was the mother of them all, and the reward of the blessed was a return ticket to it, or to someplace like it. A parody appearing during the "Me" decade in *Harper's Magazine,* an advertising campaign on behalf of the Seven Deadly Sins—Pride, Anger, Lust, Envy, Gluttony, Avarice, and Sloth (nowadays, it has been suggested, masquerading as Self-Esteem, Assertiveness, Libido, Appreciation, Gusto, Enterprise, and Stress Management)—headlined the ad for the last of these as follows: "If Sloth Had Been the Original Sin, We'd Still Be in Paradise." Islam also acknowledges seven deadly sins: deserting a pilgrimage, disobeying one's parents, murder, idolatry, usury, falsely accusing a woman of adultery, and wasting the estate of orphans.

For Christians, a specifically *celestial* Paradise was a later development, as was the idea of *Purgatory* (where one went to be purged—cleansed—of one's sins). *Heaven,* for its part, is said by some etymologists to be related to the word *camber,* 'arch, arched surface,' the reference point being to the apparent celestial dome. It is tempting to take *The Divine Comedy* at its word and forget the importance of allegory and emblem to the medieval mind: Dante's ten heavens, each higher than the last, do correspond to the Ptolemaic cosmology's nesting spheres of the moon, Mercury, Venus, the sun, Mars, Jupiter, Saturn, the Fixed Stars, and the Prime Mover—in Dante's allegory, the realms of Angels, Archangels, Principalities, Powers, Virtues, Dominations, Thrones, Cherubim, and Seraphim, respectively—with the Empyrean Heaven at the top. But the little ladder on the map between the Seventh Heaven (Saturn) and the Eighth (Fixed Stars) isn't leaning there so much as a matter of doctrine as it is an excuse for Dante to place Jacob's vision of a stairway to the sky in a Christian frame.

Dante gets to Heaven only after he and Virgil descend to the bottom of Hell and then climb the Mount of Purgatory. But back when Virgil wrote the *Aeneid,* Purgatory wouldn't yet have been there to climb: As a concept it originated only by the third century A.D., and was not fully refined till over a millennium later.

The idea that some sins were redeemable after death began early in popular Christianity in prayers and actions taken on behalf of the dead, called *suffrages*. The Church Fathers, pressed to seek scriptural justification for such beliefs and behaviors, were able to find four: Judas Maccabeus's sacrifice after battle to redeem the souls of his slain troops, an allusion in the Gospel of Matthew to the remission of sins in another world, Paul's reference to purification of sinners after death "as if by fire," and the parable Jesus told of the rich man and poor Lazarus, as recounted by Luke.

In his *Summa Theologica*, written a generation before Dante, Thomas Aquinas formulated what one writer (Brian Hayes, in the "Computer Recreations" column of the December 1983 issue of *Scientific American*) has described as a finite-state model of the soul.

A finite-state machine is one that works by accepting input items in sequence, and potentially transferring from one state to another based on the input item and the current state. The coin-counting mechanism in a vending machine is a finite-state machine. Initially, the machine is in the "no money" state. When you insert a quarter, the machine switches to the "twenty-five cents" state. After you've put in enough money, the machine reaches the "enough money" state, from which subsequently inserted coins are ignored. If the machine is functioning properly, they are returned to you and the machine remains in the " enough money" state. When you choose a beverage, the machine swallows the money, dispenses your choice, and resets the finite-state coin counter to the "no money" state.

Finite-state machines, fundamental to the automatic translation and interpretation of languages used by computer programmers, can accept a limited set of inputs, and as the name implies, allow only a limited number of states. If the vending machine supplies cola and diet cola, but accepts quarters only, then its set of inputs has three members: a quarter, a cola selection, and a diet cola selection. If drinks cost seventy-five cents, the machine has four states: "no money," "twenty-five cents," "fifty cents," and "enough money."

In baseball, the "count" of balls and strikes during a particular batter's appearance at the plate is another example of a finite-state machine. The possible inputs are: ball, strike, foul ball, fair ball, and *hit batsman* (i.e., the batter is struck by a pitch). The possible states are the possible counts: "no balls and no strikes," "one ball and no strikes,'' and so on up to ''three balls and two strikes,'' the aptly named *full count*.

When it receives an input item (a coin for the vending machine, a pitch for the baseball count), the finite-state machine chooses a subsequent state based on both the input and the current state. For example, the vending machine grants a cola only if you request it while the machine is in the ''enough money'' state. Similarly, at a count of ''one ball and one strike,'' a foul ball changes the count to ''one ball and two strikes,'' because a foul ball counts as a strike against the batter. However, a subsequent foul ball does not change the count, because a batter's third strike cannot be a foul ball (unless it's a bunt).

The soul, created in a state of risk (thanks to Original Sin), enters a state of grace upon baptism. (The term *grace* is from Latin *grātia,* 'favor; pleasure; thanks.' It is in the first sense that Christians speak of a state of grace—and in the last that they ''say grace'' before meals.) But because it has free will, the soul is at liberty to sin. (The term *sin* comes from a common Germanic form whose ultimate origin is the Indo-European root used to express the notion of 'being, existence' that shows up in English *sooth* and *essence,* the Romance languages to express the idea of transgression having gone with Latin *peccātum,* from the verb *peccāre* 'to stumble, sin,' and the basis of *peccadillo.*) After baptism, committing a mortal sin (such as premeditated murder) switches the soul from grace to the state of mortal sin (so called because it spells the death of the soul). Committing a venial sin in a state of grace switches to a state of venial sin (so called from Latin *venia* 'forgiveness, indulgence,' the idea being that venial sins are ultimately forgivable even if you die with them on your soul). But committing a venial sin in a state of mortal sin leaves you in a state of mortal sin; the soul does not change states. (If it did, the state of your soul would depend on the severity of your most recent sin only.)

Either of two inputs may be sufficient to effect a change from a state of venial sin back to a state of grace: Performing an Act of Contrition or making Confession. Making Confession may suffice to effect a change from a state of mortal sin back to a state of grace (though this is obviously not a possibility if the sin was suicide). The final earthly input is death, which leads to salvation (from a state of grace), Purgatory (from a state of venial sin), or eternal damnation (from a state of mortal sin). The final input of all is Last Judgment, which leads to damnation (from the state of damnation) or salvation (from the state of salvation, purgatory, or, until this century, limbo).

Limbo—a Late Latin term meaning, originally, 'border,' the idea being that Limbo bordered on Hell—was thought to be a dim evening-all-afternoon place where nothing much happened to you, good or bad—not all that different from Sheol, or from the middle ground of the Greek underworld, *Hades*—"the easiest room in Hell," as one Puritan divine appealingly described it. Medieval theologians came up with the idea of Limbo to handle the troublesome case of children who died before they could be baptized: They hadn't sinned yet, but they were in a state of sin anyway, on account of being progeny of Adam and Eve. Limbo also served as the abode of virtuous pagans who lived before the advent of Christianity, which is why Dante met Virgil there. Eventually, the Roman Catholic Church rethought the matter and concluded that Limbo was unnecessary and, in this century, abolished it.

In both the Roman Catholic Church and the Islamic faith, seven is the age of reason. Muslims below that age are not expected to observe the rituals of prayer and fasting that form a normal part of the adult practitioner's life; and Catholic children first take Communion at seven, after which they are expected to attend Mass regularly, observe Holy Days of Obligation, and go to Confession, being held accountable for their sins. We know of one five-year-old Catholic girl so impressed by the age of reason, she uttered this birthday wish to her seven-year-old brother: "Happy birthday, Matthew. Now you can go to Hell."

The seven-year intervals of human life are sometimes called the *climacterics,* from Greek *klimax* ('ladder') in the sense that each such year is another rung up. We are "reasonable" children at seven, reach puberty at fourteen, are considered to be old enough to drink, fight in the army, and vote by twenty-one. True, perhaps the fit isn't always exact: Better nutrition in a society means that girls reach puberty earlier; in the United States, draft age was eighteen, to which the voting age was lowered during the Vietnam War, as was the drinking age in some states that later thought better of it and raised it to twenty-one again.

Since nine was also thought to be a significant interval, the *Grand Climacteric,* sixty-three (7×9), was especially portentous: In Greco-Roman folklore, life was nine sevens, and then you died. Even today, despite our propensity to measure time after adolescence by decades (*thirtysomething,* "Life begins at forty," and chain-store *Half-Century Club* discount cards), sixty-three still matters: Social Security kicks in at different levels bracketing this age, and the next climacteric (7×10) is the Bible's "threescore and ten," the measure of a long life.

The seven-year interval has also found its way into the folk psychology of marital relations as "the seven-year itch." Counting from the year of marriage, the seventh year does seem to be a point at which, if something can go wrong, it will. Women who married expecting to have children as soon as it's possible (financially, emotionally, geographically) might begin to wonder if they've been had; their husbands may fantasize about, or actually wander off seeking, younger bedmates; and whatever reservoir of goodwill got the couple past the first year or two can seem to have gone bone-dry. It is not the only climacteric within marriage (fourteen or so and twenty-one or so also yield spikes, or at least bumps, in the statistical curve of divorce) but it is the first and perhaps the scariest.

Middle age too has its climacteric years: It is not for nothing that *climacteric* is a synonym for *menopause.* As the Chinese noted, the age range of forty-five to fifty-four during which most women experience it centers on forty-nine (7×7). In Sweden, in contrast to our retirement-with-full-benefits-at-sixty-five celebrations, the tradition is to give the gold watch—and a banquet—at fifty-five, when one is presumably at the height of status and not yet noticeably declining in social power or bodily vigor, or at least is still expected at work the next day. Like sixty-five, this is ostensibly a five-year milestone, but it may be no coincidence that it is also the year leading up to the eighth climacteric, fifty-six.

The number 56, incidentally, has another interesting property in which seven might be said to have a shadowy presence, namely: 56 is the sum of two three-digit *rep-numbers*, that is, numbers that can be represented as a string of 1's in some base systems— $56_{decimal} = 111_{base3} + 111_{base6}$, that is, $56 = 13 + 43$. Where does seven come into this? Seven is the first number that can be represented numerically as 111 (in base 2).

Schematically, rep-numbers can be represented as trees whose forks have the same number of branches. Here's 7 in base 2, i.e., $2^0 + 2^1 + 2^2$:

Figure 12: A Seven Tree

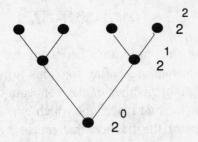

and here's 13 in similar clothing ($3^0 + 3^1 + 3^2$):

Figure 13: A Thirteen Tree

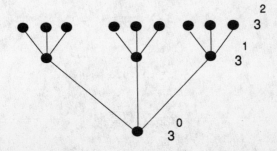

and 21 ($4^0 + 4^1 + 4^2$):

Figure 14: A Twenty-One Tree

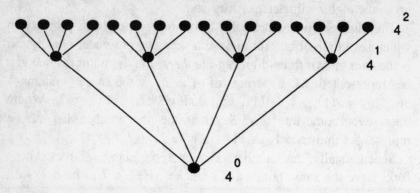

If 7/1 yields a repeating series of 1's in base 2, 1/7 yields what's known as a *repeating fraction*. In base 10:

$$\frac{1}{7} = .142857142857\overline{142857}$$

This is a repeating fraction with a period of six digits. It is convenient shorthand to mark repeating fractions (especially ones with long periods) in one or another of the conventional ways that are still slugging it out for first place, for which our vote is for putting a bar over the part of the fraction that repeats, as we have done above.

That said, consider the following:

$$\frac{2}{7} = .\overline{285714}$$

$$\frac{3}{7} = .\overline{428571}$$

$$\frac{4}{7} = .\overline{571428}$$

$$\frac{5}{7} = .\overline{714285}$$

$$\frac{6}{7} = .\overline{857142}$$

These six repeating decimals have the same six numbers in the same order—for example, 1 always follows 7 and precedes 4.

When you add ⅐ (.1428571 . . .) to ⁶⁄₇ (.8571428 . . .), you get .9999999 . . . , that is, 1.

What's going on here? First, realize that a rational number is the quotient of two integers, and ⅐ is just such a division, as are ¼ and ³⁄₁₁. You can find the decimal expansion of such a fraction by performing the long division, during the individual steps of which three possible things can happen: (1) No remainder. You're done. For example,

$$\frac{1}{4} = 4\overline{\smash)\begin{array}{r} 0.25 \\ 1.00 \end{array}}$$
$$\underline{8}$$
$$20 \text{ ("2" is the remainder.)}$$
$$\underline{20}$$
$$0 \text{ ("0" is the remainder, so you're done.)}$$

(2) A remainder you've seen before. You're done, because you can now read the pattern of repeating digits in the answer. For example,

$$\frac{3}{11} = 11\overline{\smash)\begin{array}{r} 0.27 \\ 3.00 \end{array}}$$
$$\underline{22}$$
$$80$$
$$\underline{77}$$
$$3 \text{ (This is where we came in;}$$
$$\text{the answer is } .\overline{27})$$

or (3) A remainder you haven't seen before. Keep going.

In the keep-going case, you should not lose heart: When you're dividing by 7, for example, there are only six possible nonzero remainders that could appear. Ideally, you'll eventually get a remainder of 0. At worst, you'll come to a remainder you've seen before, after calculating the quotient to no more than six places.

When dividing by 7, the worst possible case comes true: You will cycle through all six possible remainders before encountering a repeater. Hence, the repeating decimal for ⅐ has six digits in it.

Fractions like $\frac{1}{7}$, whose long divisions generate the maximum number of possible remainders, are called *full repetend fractions*. Whether a fraction is a full repetend fraction or not depends on what base system you're in: $\frac{1}{7}$ in base 10 is a full repetend fraction, but not in base 7 (because in base 7, one seventh is written "0.10").

After $\frac{1}{7}$, the next full repetend fraction in base 10 is $\frac{1}{17}$. The period of this decimal is 16 digits long, because every possible remainder appears in the long division. Here are the fractions for $\frac{1}{17}$, $\frac{8}{17}$, and $\frac{9}{17}$:

$$\frac{1}{17} = 0.\overline{058,823,529,411,764,7}$$

$$\frac{8}{17} = 0.\overline{470,588,235,294,117,6}$$

$$\frac{9}{17} = 0.\overline{529,411,764,705,882,3}$$

The sum of $\frac{8}{17}$ and $\frac{9}{17}$ is .999,999,999,999,999,9 . . . , as it should be: God's in His Heaven; all's right with the world.

EIGHT

"Behind the eight ball," we say, to describe the unenviable position of someone in line for big trouble. The metaphor is from the billiard parlor, and refers to the rules in standard pool that restrict when you can strike or sink the black eight ball: If it blocks the path of your shot, you must find an alternate route.

The standard billiard table in America is 4 feet 6 inches by 9 feet. This proportion of 1:2 also holds for carom and snooker tables, which are 5 feet by 10 feet. The preferred height is 31 to 32 inches. Probably invented in France during the reign of Louis XI (1461–1483), billiards first gained acceptance at the court of Charles IX, who was playing the game by 1571.

The word *billiards* derives from French *bille* '(cue) stick,' originally 'tree trunk.' (The medieval Latin words *billus* and *billa*, probably of Celtic origin, meant 'branch, trunk,' a sense preserved in English *billet* 'piece of firewood,' thence 'bar of iron or steel in a middle phase of its fabrication.') *Bille* came to be used for '(pool) table' as well as '(pool) cue.' Possibly influenced by another *bille* 'little ball' (from Latin *pila),* the game got called *billards* in French and was imported into English as *billiards*.

To this day a French euphemism for 'to die' (similar to *cash in one's chips*) is *dévisser son billard,* literally, 'unscrew one's cue stick.' The *cue* of the pool hall is unrelated to the *cue* of the stage—whose origin is obscure—but identical with the *queue* at the British box office: Both are from French *queue* 'tail,' used figuratively for 'stick.'

The cue was introduced in 1735 in France, prior to which balls were propelled by a small mace. A certain Captain Mingaud, jailed under political displeasure in 1798, whiled away his time in prison modifying the cue; he added the leather tip. Chalk came into use later thanks to Jack Carr, a British billiards virtuoso of the 1800s, who is also credited with originating a set of "English" shots, a term later borrowed into several other sports as a synonym for the spin a player puts on the ball.

While most Americans think of *billiards* as a fancy word for *pool,* scholars of the game distinguish among several games in the billiards family, pool being only one of them. The name *pool* has nothing to do with water, but is from French *poule* 'game, stake, pot'—literally, 'hen.' Was a chicken in every pot? Not quite: In the game of *poule,* anybody who wanted to bet on the game could pony up, winner take all. It has been suggested that the pile of coins in the middle of a table may have reminded many players of a clutch of eggs under a hen. English retains this sense of pool in *typing pool, pool our resources,* and, for Britons especially, *football* [i.e., *soccer*] *pool.*

To *pony up* may be from Latin *pōne*—not the adverb and preposition meaning 'after, behind' (although this is the source for the *pony* in poker, the person to the dealer's right), but from the verb *pōnere* 'to place, lay (down).' In England, rents and other obligations were discharged quarterly, and the first of the days that marked the beginning of the four quarters in the year was March 25—"Lady Day," the feast of the Annunciation. It was not until the adoption of the Gregorian calendar in 1752 that the English moved the beginning of the year from March 25 to January 1. In the Anglican church, the psalm appointed to be read on the twenty-fifth of the month is #119—#118 in the Vulgate—whose thirty-third verse reads "*Lēgem pōne mihi, Domine, viam iustificātiōnum tuārum, et exquīram eam semper*" ('Teach me, O Lord, the way of thy statutes, and I shall keep it unto the end.') So *legem pōne*—literally, 'lay down the law'—came to be used facetiously for 'ready money,' since the day that psalm was read in church at the beginning of the year was the day everybody had to have some.

Ponying up appears to have no connection with the *pony* that is a little horse, which is derived from a diminutive of medieval French *poulain* 'foal' from Latin *pullus* 'young animal,' which is ultimately from the same root as the *ped-* of Greek *pedagogy* and *pedophilia* and is related to Latin *paucus* 'small,' *pauper* 'poor,' *puer* 'boy,' and *puella* 'girl,' as well as *pusillus* 'very tiny'—whence came (with *anima* 'soul') English *pusillanimous* 'faint-spirited, cowardly.' *Pullus* is also, as it happens, the direct ancestor of *poule*.

The rules for pool as played in America are familiar enough that we need not repeat them here. Instead, here are some of the other forms of billiards, roughly in chronological order of appearance.

Nowadays we use the word *carom* in the loose sense of 'ricochet,' but the word actually comes from an early French version of billiards called *carambolage*. *Carambole* is from Spanish/Portuguese *carambola,* itself from Marathi *karambal* ('fruit of the *Averrhoa carambola'*), whose origin is Sanskrit *karmaphala* 'the fruit or recompense of actions (as, pain, pleasure, etc.) resulting from acts in a previous life' from *karma* plus *phala* 'fruit,' which shares a common Indo-European root (**bhel-*, meaning 'swell, grow') with the *phal-* of *phallus,* the *flo-* of *flower,* and the *bole* of a tree (itself possibly related to *billet*).

During their colonial inroads into southern India, the Portuguese were introduced to the *Averrhoa carambola,* whose fruit looks good but tastes bitter. The explorers brought back the name to the Iberian Peninsula as a synonym for 'trap, snare, entanglement,' from which it derived its later sense as 'cast, throw, move (in a game),' adopted by the French to refer specifically to 'billiards shot in which the cue ball hits two other balls,' its sense today. When English borrowed the term, it got shortened to *carom,* the game being called *carom billiards* or *canon billiards*.

Carambolage is played with three balls (two white, one red) on a table with no pockets. The first player shoots with the intention of hitting first a red ball and then a white one with one shot using the other white ball. Assuming success, that player can continue shooting as long as he hits both balls (in either order) with each shot. Each successful shot adds to his score. When he misses, the other player takes over. The game is played until some previously agreed-upon number of points has been scored by the winner. A carom table is also suitable for *three-cushion billiards,* in which, as the name implies, the player must make the shot such that the cue ball bounces three times off the side felt before striking its target.

A variant: *partie de cinq quilles,* or 'pin pool.' The same rules hold as for carambolage, with the added wrinkle that a pin is stuck upright into the middle of the table and four others are arranged around it such that a ball can barely pass between any two pins. The idea is to knock down the pins by making one of your two object balls rebound off a cushion. The four outer pins are worth a point each and the inner one, if knocked down without touching the outside ones, is worth five. If you knock any of the pins down with your own cue ball, however, your opponent gets your accumulated points. This game is usually played up to a score of fifty. Pin pool is probably the ancestor of *bumper pool,* imported to America by returning GIs. Its popularity was enhanced by its smaller—3 feet by 6 feet—table, which could fit more easily into postwar suburban rumpus rooms.

In its classic form, *poule* is played on a table with pockets and just two balls, both white. (One has a red dot on it so you can tell which is which.) As many players as want to be in the game draw numbers to determine the order of play. This used to be done using little spheres with numbers on them, shaken in a basket and then drawn, one by each player—a possible origin for the numbered balls used in standard American pool today. Player number one and player number two then take turns trying to knock each other's ball in (without accumulating negative points, as when your own ball goes in the pocket).

The first player whose ball gets sunk loses the round and earns a negative point; the winner of that round then plays the next player in line, the winner of that round plays the next in line, and so on. Three negative points and you're "dead," i.e., out of the game; and the game is over when there is only one player left, all others being "dead."

There are both British and American varieties of snooker (a term of obscure origin), the Yankee version being played with a rack of twenty-one balls—fifteen red and six colored. The red ones each count for a point; the colored ones are numbered 1 through 6, corresponding to the number of points each is worth. To snooker someone is to get the better of him, as when the unsuspecting rube is persuaded to part with his money in a series of friendly games with the pool hall's resident shark.

Pool requires a smooth flat playing surface and near-perfect spheres for the balls. Many players prefer a tabletop made of slate (which fractures into thin even planes) with felt over it. Billiard balls used to be milled out of ivory; nowadays they're made of phenolic resin, a hydrocarbon polymer, cast into spherical molds.

The volume of a sphere, such as a billiard ball, is four-thirds the cube of its radius times pi, or $4\pi r^3/3$. *Cube?* The exponential powers x^2 and x^3 are called the *square* and *cube* of x because it is easy to visualize them as x extended in two and three dimensions. Even though we have a name for a four-dimensional hypercube, nobody ever says "x tesseracted" for x^4, though presumably one could. We just say "x to the fourth power," or "x to the fourth."

Cubed and *squared* are terms that we have inherited from the study of the so-called *figurate* numbers, that is, whole numbers that can be represented as regular geometric figures—for example, a square number is one that can be represented as a square array of units (pebbles, having been the preferred unit among the Pythagoreans):

Figure 15: Square Numbers

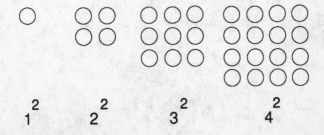

$$1^2 \qquad 2^2 \qquad 3^2 \qquad 4^2$$

The square numbers are 1, 4, 9, 16, 25, 36 . . . (i.e., 1^2, 2^2, 3^2, 4^2, 5^2, 6^2 . . .), the nth term in the series being simply n^2. Pythagoras was definitely familiar with square numbers and he may also have known about triangular numbers—those in which each row has one more pebble than the row next to it: $1 + 2 + 3 + \ldots + n$. This sequence goes 1, 3, 6, 10, 15, 21 . . . .

Figure 16: Triangular Numbers

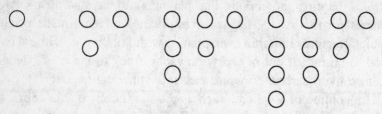

Note that the fifth term is 15, i.e., $1 + 2 + 3 + 4 + 5$. Instead of pebbles in the sand, imagine fifteen billiard balls in a triangular rack. For another triangular number, ten, imagine the configuration of pins in bowling.

Figure 17: Ten Pins

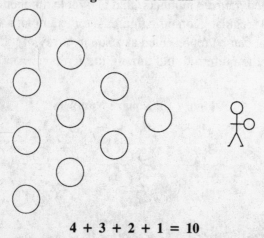

$$4 + 3 + 2 + 1 = 10$$

The old style of bowling used nine pins, a square number; arranged in a 3×3 array with a corner toward the bowler. And in nine-ball billiards, the balls are racked in a rhombus.

Figure 18: Nine Ball Billiards Rack

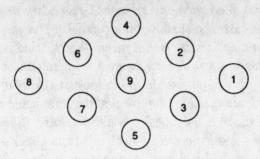

Pythagoras recognized a curious fact about the square numbers: The nth square is the sum of the first n odd numbers. For example: $4^2 = 1 + 3 + 5 + 7$. Here's what's going on spatially:

Figure 19: L Squares

○	○	○	○	1
○	○	○	○	3
○	○	○	○	5
○	○	○	○	7

———

16

Because of their potential arrangement into an L shape, the odd numbers were called *gnomons,* from the Greek name for the L-shaped indicator that casts the shadow on a sundial. (The *gno-* is the same one in *agnostic* and *gnosticism;* it means 'know,' and is its cognate.)

Now Pythagoras was already aware that the relationship of the two shorter sides of a right triangle to the longest side is $a^2 + b^2 = c^2$ where a and b are the sides that meet at the right angle that *subtends* (i.e., is opposite to and defines) c, the *hypotenuse*. (*Subtend*—which is from Latin—and *hypotenuse*—which is from Greek—derive from cognate verbs meaning, literally, 'to stretch under.') This is called the Pythagorean theorem, because, while it may have been discovered earlier and elsewhere, it was Pythagoras and his school who first put this formula on the charts of Math's Greatest All-Time Hits, right up there with $a = \pi r^2$, the equation for determining the area of a circle from its radius.

Figure 20: A Gnomon

Pythagoras also knew that $3^2 + 4^2 = 5^2$. He searched for other number triads like (3, 4, 5) that stood in this relationship. Here, focusing on the gnomon yields the answer; if the gnomon is a square number, we're in business. If the gnomon (shaded in Figure 20) is a square number, we can find the sides of other Pythagorean triangles—other numbers satisfying $a^2 + b^2 = c^2$.

Figure 21: The Pythagorean Theorem in Mufti

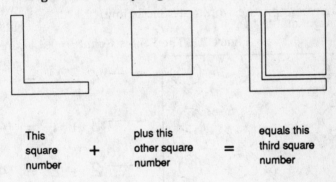

This square number   **+**   plus this other square number   **=**   equals this third square number

For example, if the gnomon is 9 (3^2), the square that it cradles is 16 (4^2), and the square that they make when you put them together is 25 (5^2); if the gnomon is 25 (5^2), the square that it cradles is 144 (12^2), and the square that they make when you put them together is 169 (13^2); and so on.

. . . and the Pythagorean theorem is satisfied.

Another way of looking at square numbers is as the sum of two consecutive triangular numbers. For example, $10 + 6 = 16$.

Figure 22: A Triangular Square

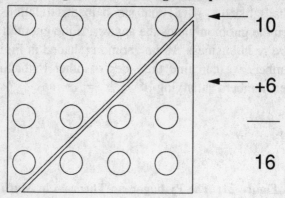

How does the picture work out? See below.

Figure 23: The Pebble Count

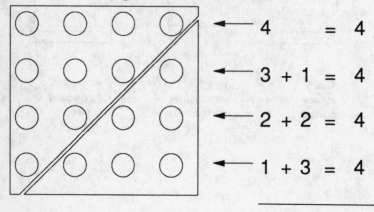

There are other polygons besides triangles and squares. Accordingly, there are other sets of figurate numbers. The pentagonal numbers, for example, are 1, 5, 12, 22 . . . ; the nth pentagonal number is the sum of the first n terms of this series:

$$1 + 4 + 7 + 10 + 13 + \ldots$$

Each sequence of figurate numbers is based on a different shape, and each sequence starts with 1 and expands through gnomons with a fixed number of ever-lengthening legs: The triangular numbers expand through one-legged gnomons, the square numbers expand through gnomons with two legs, the pentagonal numbers expand through gnomons with three legs, and so on. Each sequence starts with 1 because that's the number of pebbles left when you peel away all of its surrounding gnomons.

Figure 24: Gnomons

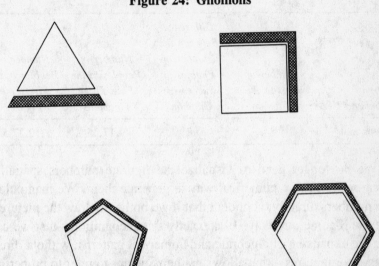

Now we've established a pattern, which we can summarize.

Type of Number	Number of Legs in the Gnomon	Difference Between the Number of Pebbles in Successive Gnomons	Number of Pebbles in Each of the First Three Gnomons	Number of Pebbles in the First Four Figures
Triangular	1	1	2,3,4	1,3,6,10
Square	2	2	3,5,7	1,4,9,16
Pentagonal	3	3	4,7,10	1,5,12,22
Hexagonal	4	4	5,9,13	1,6,15,28

In the preceding table, the two leftmost columns refer to the shapes of the figurate numbers themselves, showing how the pictures reveal the pattern. The other columns describe the same figures, only arithmetically. At this point, we can detect the numerical pattern from the table. Appreciating this pattern, we can immediately write the eighth row of the table, about decagonal (i.e., ten-sided) numbers and can skip the intermediate rows containing the seven-, eight-, and nine-sided figurate numbers.

Type of Number	Number of Legs in the Gnomon	Difference Between the Number of Pebbles in Successive Gnomons	Number of Pebbles in the First Three Gnomons	Number of Pebbles in the First Four Figures
Decagonal	8	8	9,17,25	1,10,27,52

We no longer need to visualize the figurate numbers spatially, because we have a numerical way to generate them. We manipulate the numbers directly, confident that if we bother to draw the pictures, they will come out okay. It is exactly this recognition—that we can use the expansion of algebraic and numerical patterns, without direct regard for pictures—that allows mathematicians to refer to properties of things they have never *seen*. In fact, it is such algebraic patterns that let mathematicians talk about impossible, seemingly crazy stuff like four-dimensional space.

We've seen it once already in this chapter. If x is a number, then x^2 is a square, x^3 is a cube, x^4 is a four-dimensional hypercube (tesseract), and x^5 is a five-dimensional hypercube. Here, the algebraic pattern is simple: To move to the next higher dimension, increase the exponent by one.

The series of cubic numbers, or perfect cubes, begins 1, 8, 27, 64, 125 . . . (1^3, 2^3, 3^3, 4^3, 5^3, . . .). The first three are illustrated graphically, on the next page.

Figure 25: Cubes

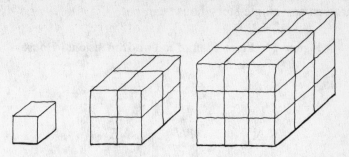

The series of four-dimensional hypercubic numbers begins 1, 16, 81, 256, 625, . . . (1^4, 2^4, 3^4, 4^4, 5^4, . . .). We can illustrate, albeit metaphorically, a four-dimensional hypercube. Imagine that you live in a bizarre land with many dimensions but restrictive zoning laws. The laws limit how long, wide, or tall your house can be, with a two-room limit in every direction. However, the law says that your house can span as many dimensions as you wish.

The typical starter home has two rooms, side by side. This house is as wide as allowable by law. Caveat emptor: The following floor plan of a typical starter home falsely suggests that the rooms have depth as well as width, which, by definition, they don't—a fact that the realtor would prefer to ignore until the question of where to put your grand piano comes up to force the issue.

Figure 26: Floor Plan of a One-Dimensional House

Having been euchred into buying a starter home, you can enlarge the house into the second dimension, adding two more rooms behind the first two (which can now quietly assume the depth of the other two while nobody's looking). Now the house has four rooms, and is as large as any single-story house can be.

Figure 27: Floor Plan of a Two-Dimensional House

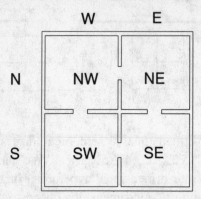

You discover that there is a zoning law of which you were unaware, which requires each room in a house to have direct access to all of its adjacent rooms. In the two-room house, a doorway connecting the two rooms satisfies this requirement. In the four-room home, each room has two doors, one leading to the adjacent room alongside (to the west or east), and one leading to the adjacent room toward the north or south.

Your four-room house exhausts the potential for expansion in the dimensions of width and depth. To enlarge again, you'll need to grow in a third direction (or dimension, if you prefer): up. You add a second story, identical to the first. Now the house has eight rooms, four on the first floor and four on the second. Each room now has three exits, one leading west or east, one leading north or south, and one leading to a staircase.

Each of the rooms in the house is identified by three variables: latitude, longitude, and elevation. Because each variable has two possible values, the rooms can be identified by a three-bit binary number, where each bit represents one of the three variables.

Figure 28: Floor Plan of a Three-Dimensional House

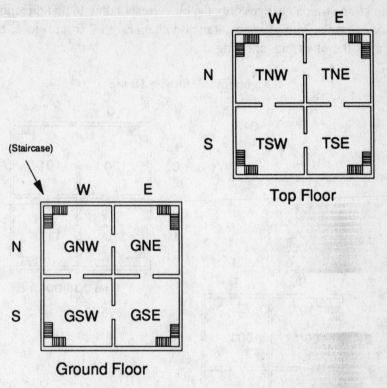

Top Floor

Ground Floor

Figure 29: Underneath the Floor Plan

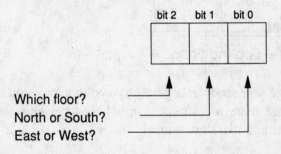

Furthermore, exiting from one room to another moves in a specific direction, which changes only the bit corresponding to that direction. For example, going up any staircase changes bit 2 from 0 to 1, but leaves the other bits unchanged.

Figure 30: A Bitwise House

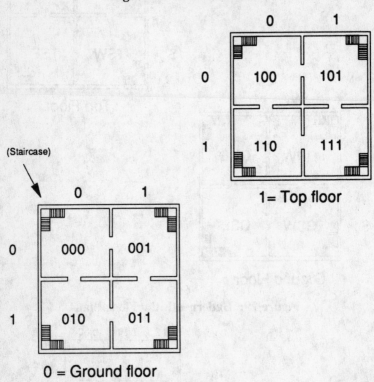

Once again, we encounter a purely symbolic expression of a spatial system. And there are similar symbolic expressions for the one-dimensional and two-dimensional houses.

Figure 31: Underneath the Two-Bit House

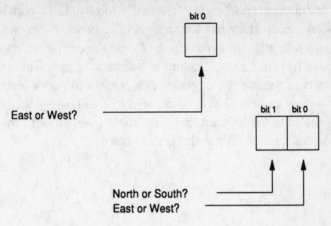

We can expand the symbolism into universes that cannot be represented spatially, such as the four-dimensional universe. In our binary symbolism, four dimensions simply means four bits in the "address" of each room. A four-dimensional house can have up to sixteen rooms and each room has four exits leading off in four different directions. Exiting from a room takes you to another whose address differs by only one bit.

Figure 32: Underneath a Four-Bit Mansion

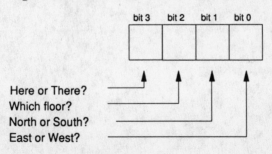

The sixteen-room house has two identical parts, the recent eight-room addition and the eight "original" rooms. Each part has two stories, and each story has four rooms. The house is two wide, two deep, two tall, and two *across in the fourth dimension*. Each room in the house has four exits, leading to adjacent rooms. The east-west door leads to the room alongside. The north-south door leads to the room in front or behind. The stairs lead to a different floor. And the trap door leads to the corresponding room *over there* in the fourth dimension where we'll put the grand piano.

NINE

NINE TAILORS MAKE A MAN is a saying that is more apt to ring a bell than conjure up an actual meaning with most contemporary speakers of English, a pretty good sign that it is on its way to the dustbin of linguistic history to join such grizzled worthies as *every mickle makes a muckle* and *twenty-three skidoo*. The expression, which has until recently been used to disparage a person's physique (formerly, and more specifically, to disparage a tailor's physique) originally seems to have referred to the practice in rural England of broadcasting the news via the church bell that a parish member had just died: When a man died, the bell was rung (or *tolled*) nine times and then once again for each year that the deceased had lived. When a woman died, the bell was rung six times before tolling the number of her years. A child's death was marked by three preliminary rings.

Happily, the law of averages limits the number of catastrophes striking a particular parish. Most inhabitants would know who was who by sex and age. But during an epidemic, with the bell tolling almost without pause, could we be sure that those nine strokes we just heard referred to a man? Or was it a child of six, and now we're on to the next casualty?

Worse, suppose so many are dying that the ringer decides to skip the age-strokes altogether. We hear eighteen strokes, indistinctly enough that we can't tell whether the village has just lost two men, or three women, or perhaps some combination that includes children. Even assuming that no child dies (it simplifies the math and makes the story gentler), there are several interpretations for most tolls.

Number of Bell Strokes	*Possible Body Count, by Sex*
24	2 men, 1 woman
	4 women
27	3 men
	1 man, 3 women
36	4 men
	2 men, 3 women
	6 women
60	6 men, 1 woman
	4 men, 4 women
	2 men, 7 women
	10 women

These ambiguities crop up less often in a system in which the numbers for men and women are relatively prime, i.e., have no shared factor. (*Relative* here means 'in relation to,' not 'somewhat.') By itself, 9 is not relatively prime: but 9 and 7 are relatively prime with respect to each other because they share no factors. The numbers 9 and 6 are not relatively prime: Both can be divided by 3. Had "man" been 9 strokes and "woman" 7, there would be no common divisor and the table would look like this:

Number of Bell Strokes	*Possible Body Count, by Sex*
7	1 woman
9	1 man
14	2 women
16	1 man, 1 woman
18	2 men
21	3 women
23	1 man, 2 women
25	2 men, 1 woman
27	3 men
28	4 women

Choosing relative primes does not eliminate all ambiguous death knells. Sixty-three (9×7) is the first (lowest) ambiguous knell: seven dead men or nine dead women. Zero strokes of the bell clapper, on the other hand, remain ambiguous in all systems. It could mean no deaths; it could mean one death (the bell ringer's); or it could mean that there were so many deaths that the ringer couldn't keep up with the current bills of mortality, so stopped ringing the bell altogether (which is what actually happened in London during the plague of 1665–1666).

So how did tailors get involved with bell ringing? Basically, the connection seems to have been a case of "take care of the sounds and the sense will take care of itself" (a saying minted by Lewis Carroll, playing on "take care of the pounds and the pence will take care of themselves"), the chief players being a handful of similar-sounding English words with decidedly different roots:

- *Tell* (past tense *told*), *tale, talk*—these come from an Indo-European root (*del-) meaning 'number, count' and by extension 'recount, relate.' Modern German *Zahl* 'number,' *zählen* 'to count, number, reckon,' and *erzählen* 'to tell, relate, narrate' are the cognates that remind us that the bank teller counts your money while the fortune teller tells you a plausible tale (and then counts your money). No bell ringing or cloth cutting here.
- *Tally* and *tailor*—plenty of cutting here: a *tally* was originally a notch cut on a stick, and a *tailor* was a cutter of cloth.
- *Toll*—as in *tollbooth* (where your money is counted, an extension of the root underlying *tell, tale, talk,* and the like) and, from a totally different root meaning 'pull, draw, attract,' *toll* (as in "Ask not for whom the bell tolls"). The folks who *toll* the bells are sometimes known as *tellers*. The conflation of *teller* with *tailor* was already complete by the late sixteenth century: Elizabeth I, receiving a party of eighteen tailors come to court for a lobbying blitz, is said to have wisecracked "Good morning, gentlemen both!"

Of all honest trades the tailor's is perhaps most compellingly occupied with the measure of humankind. "Measurements are very important," says Harry Simons, author of *The Science of Human Proportions*, demonstrating the assertion in a diagram showing twenty-five different measurement points for a man's three-piece suit (numbered *A* through *Y*—the top of the trouser inseam, appropriately enough, is *V*). No tailor, naturally, would argue with this, nor would the manufacturer of off-the-rack clothing.

On the rack, togs are classified by one or a few basic measurements, forming the basis of a variety of sizing schemes, all of which are describable as discontinuous functions. Among mathematicians, the term *function* has worn several hats since Leibniz first used it in its Latin garb—*functio, functiōnis,* literally 'the performance of an action; an action, activity'—the off-the-rack definition being something like 'a variable whose value is determined by the value of some other variable, usually written $y = f(x)$, where y (called the *dependent variable*) gets its value from x (called the *independent variable*).' Such a function is termed a *single-variable function,* meaning that it has a single independent variable. Multivariable functions differ from single-variable functions. As one might expect, multivariable functions have more than one independent variable, whose values and relationships determine the value of the dependent variable: $z = f(x, y)$ says that the value of z depends on the values of x and y in whatever relationship we have defined between them. A typical multivariable function is division, because the dependent variable (the quotient) depends on both independent variables (the dividend and the divisor).

The sizing of young children's clothes involves a simple single-variable function in which size (the dependent variable) equals the kid's age (the independent variable). As the single variable (age) increases, the size increases. However, since every parent is presumed to be flattered by the exuberant growth of an offspring, the likelihood that a six year old will need a size 8 is better than average. Men's undershirt sizing is also single-variable: the size increases directly with one dimension, the chest size.

The sizing of panty hose uses a two-variable function, the two independent variables being height and weight. The same size may fit women five feet four and 140 pounds or five feet seven and 120 pounds equally well. Sizes for garter-held stockings likewise need a spreadsheet to explain—and in any case (according to a relative who wore them most of her adult life), what fits one leg will probably not fit the other.

Women's underwear is, as might be imagined, a more complicated matter. As with panty hose, a woman uses two variables to choose a brassiere size: bust measurement and cup size. Note, however, that brassiere sizing is not a two-variable function, because the result of the calculation is not a single number or size. In fact, brassiere sizing actually uses two separate single-variable functions. The same holds for men's trousers, chosen according to waist and inseam and classified on the rack that way. (Compare with panty hose— fitted by two variables but classified on the shelf by one: the generic "size.")

European sizes differ, but insignificantly. Shoe sizes use different numbers, but still rely on one variable for the length and another for the width. Women's panty sizes are a single-variable function on either side of the Atlantic: Over there, the one variable is waist, over here, it's hips.

Surprising variables can sneak into clothing sizes. For example, a mass-market clothing manufacturer, for whom every spare inch of cloth multiplies rapidly into ells, figures size precisely and wastes little; but a higher-priced line can afford to be a little bit more generous to its pattern, given the higher markup and the probability that the wearer will pay it gladly—in part out of gratitude for a size 10 she can still fit into, rather than being rudely forced to go up to a 12. So a factor in the size of a dress is its price. All else being equal, a higher-priced dress will be labeled with a lower size.

The fact that you can buy a smaller dress if you have a fatter wallet is a long, cynical way down from Protagoras the Sophist's lofty assertion that "Man is the measure of all things." Actually, what Protagoras said, according to Plato, is ". . . *pantōn chrēmatōn anthropōn metron einai,*" literally, '. . . a human being is the measure of every thing.' (*Anthropos* was the term the Greeks used to refer to a human being of unspecified gender, much as the Romans used the term *homo*—with which they contrasted *vir* 'adult male human' and *fēmina* 'adult female human'—the Greek term for 'adult male human' being *anēr, andros* and for 'adult female human' *gynē, gynai-*

kos—the combination of which gives us the English word *androgynous* 'having characteristics of both sexes.')

The adult human is indisputably the measure of a whole lot of things. The mouthful was used as a unit of measure in ancient Egypt and survives in the New World as a *half jigger*. In French, the word for 'inch' is *pouce* (literally, 'thumb') and a *pied* is a 'foot,' i.e., a length of twelve inches, while in English a *span* is the distance between the tip of the outstretched thumb and the tip of the little finger (nine inches by convention), a *hand* (by convention, four inches) is what you use to measure horses, the *ell* (nowadays reckoned at forty-five inches) and the *cubit* (whose length varies somewhere between seventeen and twenty-six inches depending on place and time in history) both originally referred to the distance from the elbow to the end of the fingers (*ell* reflects the Germanic *el-* of *elbow,* while Latin *cubitum* 'elbow' is the parent of English *cubit* and French *coude* 'elbow'). A *fathom* (six feet) was the distance from the tip of the fingers on one hand to the tip of the fingers on the other when you stood with your arms fully extended out from your sides. Ten fingers among American children is a leg up, while three fingers (of Old Red Eye) is a stiff drink among the older set, and so it goes.

Where it goes is, as often as not, into the realm of metaphor in which we find such corporeal units of measure as the *heartbeat;* the *blink* (or *wink*) of an eye—a *twinkling* being essentially a nanowink, forty winks constituting a good nap; the *Smoot* (named for the MIT student who offered himself as a measuring stick during the measuring of the length of the Massachusetts Avenue Bridge that connects Boston to Cambridge; the Smoot may be compared to the *baby's behind*, as a comparative measure of smoothness); the *skin of one's teeth* or *no skin off one's nose; head and shoulders* (as an index of metaphorical stature); and *an arm and a leg* (never two arms and a leg, or an arm and two legs, the metaphor apparently being fairly resistant to the ups and downs of the local economy).

Architects use human forms in drawings to reinforce the numerically indicated scale. In very confusing architectural detail drawings, a humanoid can reveal which way is up, too. Similarly, museum curators use the artist's signature to find the top of an abstract painting. And our favorite: Four fingers held at arm's length subtends an angle in the sky of about 8 degrees. This estimate works for just about anybody because folks with thicker fingers tend to have longer arms; extra-thick digits don't block out more of the sky when they're at the end of an extra-long arm. If your arm were shorter but your hand no less wide, your hand would occlude more of your field of vision. Hold your hand at arm's length and gradually move it closer toward your face. As it approaches, it blocks out more and more of the background, subtending a greater and greater angle.

Of course, this man-is-the-measure stuff can go too far. A balsawood salesman of our acquaintance swears the following story is true. Sheets of balsa wood are used in industry because they can be gently bent without breaking—and they're sold to meet certain tolerances of flexibility. A large corporation purchased some sheets to be used in the parabolic frame of a satellite transmitter. Shortly after delivery, a corporate engineer complained that the sheets were not as flexible as advertised. Over the phone, he told our friend that with a load of 374 pounds, the sheets flexed only five-eighths of an inch.

In the salesman's head, alarms went off. What kind of state-of-the-art test equipment (this was an aerospace company) gives readings in reduced fractional form—and in inches rather than centimeters at that? He took a wild guess: "Why did you use a load of 374 pounds?"

The engineer answered, "That's how much Stan and I weigh."

"You're *standing* on the sheets and measuring the flex with a yardstick? That's not accurate enough! And besides, these flexibility specifications require that the weight be applied at a single point in the center of the sheet."

"That's okay—we're standing on one foot."

We never found out if that was one foot each, or if one engineer was carrying the other one.

Although these particular engineers were somewhat misguided, others have produced unexpected payoffs by rethinking the interaction of our bodies with our surrounds: Thomas McMahon and his fellow researchers at Harvard discovered that redesigning an indoor track so that it resonated "in tune" with a runner's actual rhythm not only increased athletes' speed by 5 to 15 percent but also reduced on-track injuries by four-fifths!

What about rhythms? If humans are the measure of all (or a whole lot of) things, do those things include time? Wilhelm Fliess, a Viennese nose-and-throat specialist (and friend of Sigmund Freud's for thirteen years until they quarreled irreparably in 1900), was the first to theorize that all of us (irrespective of sex) operate on two cycles at once: a male cycle of twenty-three days and a female cycle of twenty-eight. Because so many numbers could be expressed by adding or subtracting some combination of 23's and 28's, Fliess thought that 23 and 28 had magical properties. His quack tome, *Der Ablauf des Lebens: Grundlegung zur Exakten Biologie* (The Rhythm of Life: Foundations of an Exact Biology) is filled with examples of natural constants expressed in terms of 23's and 28's. Fliess failed to realize that absolutely any number can be expressed this way. That is, for any number z, the equation $z = 23x + 28y$ has a solution in integers. This property of 23 and 28, so inspiring to Fliess, is quite ordinary: Any pair of relative primes exhibits it.

There are twenty-three days between consecutive peaks of the male cycle, and twenty-eight between peaks of the female cycle. But how long between those lucky days when the male and female cycles peak simultaneously? The answer is 23×28 days, because 23 and 28 are relatively prime. (The same reason accounts for 63 being the first ambiguous bell toll at nine per man and seven per woman—9 and 7 are relatively prime and $9 \times 7 = 63$.)

At first Freud thought highly of biorhythms, but later gave up on the idea, particularly when he and Fliess were no longer friends. Nevertheless, Freud's pupil Hermann Swoboda was captivated by the notion and went on to champion it as a psychologist at the University of Vienna up until his death in 1963. To the male and female cycles Swoboda's followers have added a thirty-three-day intellectual one—33 is relatively prime to both 23 and 28—and argue that those days when the three cycles reinforce each other can be marvelous if their intersection is positive, bad when they intersect in the negative, and just plain dangerous when they cross the baseline, virtually assuring that your waking hours that day will be spent spilling your coffee, smashing your china, wrecking your car, etc., and that you'd do best just to stay in bed.

According to Fliess's predictions one might expect that beard growth would be keyed to the twenty-three-day male cycle. In fact, a 1970 paper in *Nature* plausibly demonstrates that it is much more responsive to another variable: the presence or absence of a sexual partner. The (heterosexual) scientist's principal research project required him to camp out for several weeks at a time on an island lacking women. By weighing his whiskers after each shave, he found that the daily growth of his beard declined during long stays on the island, but that his whiskers would sprout with renewed vigor when he was due to go to the mainland. He concluded that the mere expectation of female companionship was sufficient to stimulate testosterone secretion. None of which invalidates Fliess and Swoboda; but it does suggest that biorhythms don't tell us all we need to know—e.g., when to put on our Sunday clothes.

Dressed [up] to the nines, attested no earlier than the late 1700s, is of obscure derivation, though its exclusive sartorial use seems to have been a narrowing of the original *[up] to the nines,* meaning 'to the greatest degree possible' (compare with the West Coast's *to the max*). *Dressed to the nines* may be derived from Middle English *to then eyne* 'to the eyes,' to which may be compared *drunk to one's hat* (*stewed to the gills*), *armed to the teeth, head over heels in love,* and *up to one's ass in alligators.*

The whole nine yards, like *dressed up to the nines,* has at least one sartorial spin. It has been variously explained as (1) the amount of cloth required for a monk's habit or a full dress kilt, (2) the contents of a coal wagon (three sections of three cubic yards each), and (3) the capacity, again in cubic yards, of a cement-mixer truck. An Alabaman variant is *dressed to the ninepins.* This is possibly a conflation of *to the nines* and *nice* [i.e., neat, precise] *as ninepins,* which has been explained variously as (1) a corruption of *to the ninepence,* because prior to the British currency reform of 1690 a ninepence coin circulated in addition to the sixpence and threepenny bit, and was often bent and given as a love token (*neat as ninepence* is still alive and well in British English); (2) a mistranslation of French *tiré(e) à quatre épingles* ('neat as a pin,' literally, 'stretched to four pins'); and (3) a gloss on the skill required for the game of ninepins.

Ninepins are set in a three-by-three grid with one corner pointing toward the bowler, as distinct from tenpins (including candle and duckpins), which are laid out in a receding triangle, the arithmetic series $1 + 2 + 3 + 4$. An apocryphal origin given for the latter game is that the Puritans of early New England thought bowling a sinful activity, and so outlawed ninepins, whereupon some enterprising gamester thought to circumvent the letter of the new law by adding a tenth pin. In either game, it requires some precision to bowl a strike—and, on an untrue lane, perhaps also some ''English,'' which the English (including Shakespeare) call ''bias'' and regularly rely upon in the other kind of bowling, the sort Sir Francis Drake was said to be doing when the news of the approaching Armada was brought to him.

Drake's game, similar to the Italian game *bocce*, had no pins at all; instead, the object was (and still is) to bowl one's ball (called a *bowl*), closest to the *jack,* a little white ball thrown more or less in a random spot on the field. Since everybody takes turns bowling several bowls each, which are left where they stop rolling through the end of the round, it is often necessary to ''bias'' later bowls—i.e., bowl them on a curve so as to get around other players' bowls already in the way of the jack. Tudor-era players tried boring holes in the original spherical bowls and inserting plugs of iron or lead off center; today's bowl is a standardized flattened sphere (''sort of the same shape as a Gouda cheese,'' a local authority informs us).

Given that the Armada's advance was constrained by its slowest ships—great lumbering galleons heavy with troops and cannon for the land assault—and the inability of the Spanish square-riggers to make much headway upwind, whereas the little British spy cutters bringing the news of the Armada's embarkation from Spanish harbors were rigged fore and aft, and could tack with ease, Drake probably did have time to finish the game, as the story claims, while his crew, hunkered down on board and ready to set sail at a snap of the fingers, may well have whiled the time away by playing nine-men's morris on a board that looked like this:

Figure 33: Ninemen's Morris

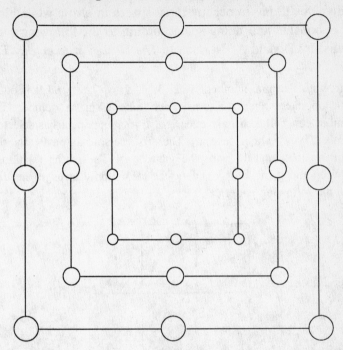

The game is for two players, each of whom has nine counters with which to try to cover any three spots or form a straight line and block the other player from doing so. Each time you make a line of three, you get to take one of your opponent's counters (as in checkers). Apparently the *morris* part of *ninemen's morris* is the same as the *morris* of *morris dance,* a traditional English dance form involving sometimes nine but more often six or eight dancers plus a fool figure, a hobbyhorse, at least one musician, and vast quantities of beer. The origin of the term *morris* is murky, though the game was also known as *merelles* to which may be compared French *marelle* 'hopscotch,' from Latin *merellus/marellus* 'counter.'

Whether ninemen's morris was the parent or merely the more sophisticated sibling of the game tic-tac-toe is not clear, though the nineness of the playing field is clear enough, and while we tend to think of tic-tac-toe as a binary sort of thing—you're either an *X* or an

O—you can just as well play the game (which, like ninemen's mor-ris, involves trying to occupy three spaces in a row while blocking your opponent from doing so) according to the following rules ar-ticulated by Donald A. Norman in *The Design of Everyday Things*:

> Start with the nine numbers 1, 2, 3, 4, 5, 6, 7, 8, and 9. You and your opponent alternate turns, each time taking a number. Each number can be taken only once, so if your opponent has selected a number, you cannot take it. The first person to have any three numbers that total 15 wins the game. . . . To see the relationship between the game of 15 and tic-tac-toe, simply arrange the digits into the following pattern:

8	1	6
3	5	7
4	9	2

. . . Any three numbers that solve the 15 problem also solve tic-tac-toe. And any tic-tac-toe solution is also a solution to 15.

All well and good but pallid in comparison to a game of baseball, in which the number 9 is preeminent, to put it mildly: The two opposing teams each consist of nine players (though the American League allows for a tenth—the *designated hitter*—who can stand in for one or another of the canonical nine when it would otherwise be that person's turn to bat).

Each team gets nine times to bat and nine times to be in the field while the other team is at bat, which is to say that the game goes for nine innings unless (1) extra innings are required to break a tie; or (2) inclement weather forces a premature end to the game (in which case, if the losing team has been at bat for at least five innings, the game is scored as though it had gone the full nine innings; otherwise the game is resumed when the weather improves); or (3) one of the teams scheduled to play doesn't show up, in which case the team that *does* show up is credited with having won the game 9 to 0.

Nine's appeal is by no means restricted to the inventors and players of games of strategy and skill like ninepins, ninemen's morris, tic-tac-toe, and baseball: The number's qualifications as three times three and as one less than ten have assured it steady employment among mystics, mythologists, and just plain folks since time immemorial. There were nine Nagas or serpents in Hindu mythology; the Jains hold that all objects fall into nine categories. The ancient oracle of Gaul was served by nine virgin priestesses (possibly surviving into Breton folklore of the last century as the *neuf corrigans* or 'Nine Fays'). The Hydra had nine heads. Deucalion's ark rode the water for nine days and nights (to Noah's—and the earlier Uta-Napishtim the Distant's—forty). And when Vulcan was thrown out of heaven, it took him nine days to tumble to earth—a detail apparently recycled by Milton when he says of the rebel angels in *Paradise Lost* (vi:870) "nine days they fell." The Nine Worthies (three pagan, three Jewish, three Christian) and Nine Virtuous Women were renowned during the waning of the Middle Ages, not to mention the Nine Muses, familiar to Greek and Roman alike.

The ninth day before the middle of the Roman month was known as the *nones* (Latin *nōnae*). Since the length of the month varied, midmonth—the *ides* (Latin *idūs*)—fell variously on the thirteenth or fifteenth day after day one—the *kalends,* so called because that was the day the priests would announce (*calāre*) when that month's ides (and therefore the nones) were going to fall. (To most citizens this probably came as no surprise: Although Roman commerce lacked the equivalent of our pocket calendars, with tide tables and advertising on them, literate Romans had presumably read their Varro and Ovid and knew the calendar pretty well already.)

The ninth hour of the Roman day, counting from dawn (the length of the hour varying somewhat with the season) was the time at which official business concluded for the day and prostitutes were allowed to come forth and offer their favors for sale in the streets in accordance with the aedile's regulations; in consequence they were called *nōnāriae*, 'ladies of the ninth hour.'

The first reference to a *nine days' wonder* is in the Roman historian Livy; its use in English—already quite current by Shakespeare's day—was certainly reinforced from the nine-day length of religious festivals during the Middle Ages—the same nine days hidden in *novena,* literally, 'a nine-day devotion,' which puts us in mind of the story of the lumber-truck driver who one day couldn't resist swiping a few things off the back for his own domestic wants. Being devout, however, at the end of the week he confessed it to his priest who, hearing that it was only the first time, only told him to say the rosary once and pray for the priest's intentions. But alas! our man was tempted again the following week, and when he came to Confession next Saturday the priest was very stern with him, saying, "Now this is the second time and I can't let you off so easy. Do you know how to make a novena?" "No," replied the miscreant, "but if you've got the plans I've got the lumber."

The human gestation period is nine months, more or less. This gets alluded to in many a song and story: "The Miller so pleased her that scarce nine months after/Her belly was filled as well as her sack," or "From October to June/She was quite out of tune/'Tis but a wanton trick" (both from D'Urfey's eighteenth-century *Wit and Mirth or Pills to Purge Melancholy*).

Premature children have, of course, been born throughout recorded history. Even primitives and pagans knew how to count, and Suetonius records that notwithstanding the official version of the event ("a miracle"), the following snappy epigram went the rounds in Rome when Decimus Drusus was born three months after his mother Livia's marriage to Augustus Caesar: "How fortunate the parents are for whom/The child is only three months in the womb." Drusus was no less fortunate, growing up to be an outstanding commander who extended Roman territory deep into the German forests and earned himself a consulship; but in 9 B.C. he was poisoned and died at his summer headquarters (thereafter known as "The Accursed Camp") when his son, the future emperor Claudius, was a mere babe in arms, so one might say that his luck—or his planets—failed him in the end.

As our highest numeral, nine is as appealing to accountants as it is to artists and social critics. The *Rule of Nine:* Numbers whose digits add up to a multiple of 9 are multiples of 9. A corollary: *casting out nines,* a method of checking addition. In a nutshell, casting out nines ensures that both sides of an equation produce the same remainder when divided by nine. For example, $548 + 79 = 627$. Divided by nine, the sum yields a remainder of 6 (9 goes into 627 69 times, with 6 remaining). The individual *summands* ('things-to-be-added'), 548 and 79, yield remainders of 8 and 7, respectively. Added together, these two remainders (from the summands' division) equal 15, whose digits add up to 6, the remainder of the sum's division.

Things are unremarkable so far: The expressions on opposite sides of an equal sign *had darn well better* act alike when divided by nine. After all, they're supposed to be equal. The benefit of casting out nines lies in the shortcut—the quick way to determine a number's remainder when dividing by nine. Start by crossing off ("casting out") nines. For example, you can quickly see that 79 leaves a remainder of 7: After you cross off the 9, 7 is what's left. Another example: 294 leaves a remainder of 6 because after you cross off the 9, 2 and 4 remain and they add up to six. What about 67,893? Start by crossing off the 9, leaving 6,783. Now you can cross off the 6 and 3 simultaneously, *because they add up to nine.* This leaves 78. Add those digits, yielding 15. Add *those* digits, yielding 6, the remainder of 67,893/9. At any time, you can cross off nines, cross off combinations of digits totaling nine, or add up the remaining digits to produce a shorter, simpler number with which to continue.

True or False: $1,369 + 8,415 = 9,794$? Work on the left side first, and start by casting out nines: 136, 8,415. Then cross off two pairs, 3-6 and 4-5, yielding 1, 81. Then cross off 81, yielding 1, the remainder of the left side of the equation when divided by nine. Now cast out nines from the right side, leaving 74. Add the digits, yielding 11. Add again, yielding 2, the remainder when the right side of the equation is divided by nine. The two sides produce different remainders, so the equation is incorrect.

This works for nine only (you cannot cast out eights, or any other number), and here's why. Every power of ten can be written as a multiple of nine plus one. (10 = 9 + 1; 100 = 99 + 1; 1,000 = 999 + 1.) Thus, it is easy to see that 1,000/9 gives a remainder of one; the same goes for 100/9 or 1,000,000/9. It follows that 2,000/9 or 200/9 gives a remainder of 2. (2,000 = 999 + 999 + 2; 200 = 99 + 99 + 2.) When we want to quickly find the remainder of a number with several digits, we just consider the digits separately:

1,232 =

| 1,000 | +200 | +30 | +2 |

| 999 + 1 | +99+99+2 | +9+9+9 + 3 | + 2 |

To calculate the remainder when dividing by nine, we can remove all the parts of the number that obviously leave a remainder of zero, which leaves as the remainder 1 + 2 + 3 + 2. These summands are the digits of the original number, 1,232.

While this is a useful test, one type of addition error it won't turn up is transposition of digits. Suppose you wrote a check and had $890.33 left in your checkbook afterwards, only you goofed and recorded it at the top of the next stub as "$980.33." Half a month and a dozen checks later, you get your bank statement and are $90 off. Here casting out nines won't do any good since the digits add up to the same number—or, put another way, the error itself is a multiple of 9—as indeed all digit-transposition goofs are. That in itself swells the accountant's bag of tricks. If two supposedly equal quantities differ by a multiple of nine, look for a digit-transposition error. Or open a new checking account at a different bank and let the one with the error lie fallow.

TEN

PENTADACTYLISM—the quality of having five fingers—has been the norm among primates since the Eocene. This is an advantage to small arboreal creatures; the more fingers, the better grip and the less likelihood of falling out of trees. After the early hominids began to make their living on the grassy savannah and to walk more or less upright, those fingers came in handy for grasping things like tools—and for counting on, which we do by tens (i.e., in base 10).

Well, most of us do. The Yuki Indians of California used base 4, counting on the spaces between the fingers of one hand rather than on the fingers themselves of both hands. Tom Lehrer's song about New Math reassured the audience that base 8 is just like base 10 if you're missing two fingers. This would be called *tetradactylism,* and is the norm at the Disney studios, which ordained that Mickey Mouse and his colleagues should have hands with only three fingers and a thumb, since this made the repetitive drawing of animation cels that much easier.

However, for everyday use, base 10 is the hands-down favorite across the globe. ''There have to be ten commandments,'' says one of the characters in Umberto Eco's *Foucault's Pendulum,* ''because, if there were twelve, when the priest counts one, two, three, holding up his fingers, and comes to the last two, he'd have to borrow a hand from the sacristan.'' Many a true word is spoken in jest. The challenge in counting on one's fingers is what to do when one gets to eleven, a challenge that one wonders how the highly numerate Babylonians met, given their sexagesimal (base 60) system of reckoning. Whether or not they figured out how to count in base 60 on their fingers (the fact that 60 breaks down nicely into 10 times 6 would have helped, perhaps), the Babylonians did apparently grasp the principle of positional notation, which they were able to apply to numbers smaller than 1 in order to represent whole-number ratios as sexagesimal fractions, in which they had a respectable stab at representing the square root of 2.

Indeed, sexagesimal fractions proved so useful that they were still used in Renaissance Europe millennia later, notwithstanding the great Fibonacci's pitch for decimal fractions, which he published in 1225 at the age of fifty in a book entitled *Flos* (The Flower). The Babylonians' base 60 led them to divide the circle (and the heavens) into 360 degrees (as opposed to 100 or 1,000)—the Romans, who already subdivided the day into hours, borrowed the further subdivision of the hour into minutes (which they termed, individually, *pars minuta prima* 'first small part') and seconds (*pars minuta secunda,* 'second small part') from Greek geometers, indebted to Babylon in their turn. So clocks were bound to turn their faces away from base 10 from the start. But ten retains a curious prominence in the timekeeper's trade: for legibility and visual balance (according to the Association of Watch and Clock Collectors), ever since the 1850s most advertisements and catalogue illustrations have clock and watch faces—even digital ones—showing 10:10.

By the time Rome became an empire, Archimedes's treatise *The Sand Reckoner* had addressed the problem of nomenclature for very large numbers. For the first time it was at least possible to talk about them (and thus to think about them—a major advance, since it is very hard to imagine a thing one cannot name).

So how did the Romans compute? On their fingers—and not just addition and subtraction but multiplication as well. When counting on their fingers, the Romans conventionally represented the first nine digits on one hand (the left, which, except where noted, was held upright and flat, with the fingers together and the thumb slightly apart) as follows:

1: fifth finger bent at middle joint.
2: fourth and fifth fingers bent at middle joints.
3: third, fourth, and fifth fingers bent at middle joints.
4: third and fourth fingers bent at middle joints.
5: third finger bent at middle joint.
6: fourth finger bent at middle joint.
7: fifth finger closed over palm.
8: fourth and fifth fingers closed over palm.
9: third, fourth, and fifth fingers closed over palm.

Continuing on the left hand, the sign for 10 was the top of the second (index) finger touching the middle joint of the thumb. The signs for 11 through 19 were the sign for 10 plus the signs for 1 through 9, made at the same time on the same hand. Similarly, the signs for 1 through 9 were combined with the following:

20: thumb placed between second and third fingers with thumbnail on middle joint of second finger.
30: thumb and second finger forming a circle.
40: thumb and second finger erect and together.
50: thumb, bent at both joints, resting on palm.
60: second finger bent over thumb resting on palm as at 50.
70: first joint of second finger resting on first joint of straight thumb.
80: tip of second finger resting on first joint of thumb.
90: thumb bent over first joint of second finger.

The sign for 100 was the sign for 10, except made with the right hand, and so on through 900. The sign for 1,000 was the sign for 1 made with the right hand, and so up through 9,000. The numbers 10,000 through 90,000 were signified by touching various parts of the body with the left hand, and 100,000 through 900,000 by touching the corresponding parts of the body with the right hand. Finally, there was a sign for a million: hands clasped, fingers interlocked. All the above remained in currency well into the Renaissance; witness the following illustration from Luca Pacioli's *Summa de Arithmetica,*

Geometria, Proportioni et Proportionalita, published at the end of the fifteenth century.

Figure 34: Early Digital Reckoning

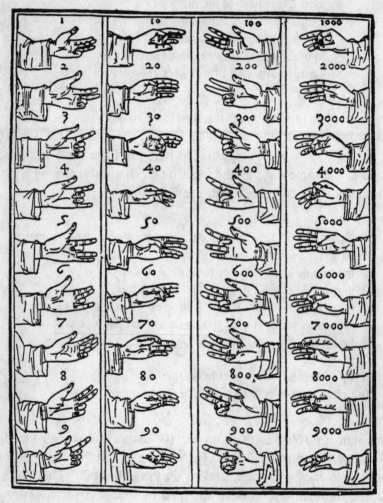

A line in Plautus's *Miles Gloriosus* (Braggart Soldier) speaks of "reckoning the pros and cons on the fingers of his right hand," a pointed suggestion that there must have been a great many of them. This figure is echoed by Juvenal felicitating Nestor, the seer of the *Iliad*, for living long enough to have to calculate the number of his years on his right hand (*suos iam dextra computat annos*). Cicero uses the phrase *si tuos digitos novi* (literally, 'if I've known your fingers') to mean 'if I know how well you calculate.' And Quintilian pleads for arithmetic literacy in the fingers of public speakers, for "if an orator's fumbling fingers are seen to stray from the normal way of calculating, it reflects badly on his training."

It seems to have been common enough, as with reading, to use one's lips, talking oneself through a computation: *Movet labra, agitat digitos, computat* ('he moves his lips; he twiddles his fingers; he calculates')—so Pliny the Younger writes of a man contemplating marriage with a rich woman. On the same theme, St. Jerome acidly observes that many men marry based on what their fingers tell them, not their eyes (*multos non oculis sed digitis uxores ducere*).

Addition and subtraction were done in the head, with the upper term displayed on the fingers and the second number being added or subtracted mentally from it, the operation being repeated as often as necessary with the result of each step displayed on the fingers in turn. How the Romans did multiplication and division is not so clear, though it's easy enough to imagine that they were familiar with a version of the system still in use in parts of Romania and rural France for multiplying two numbers between 6 and 9 on your fingers.

Here's how it works:

Let A and B be two numbers between 6 and 9.	Suppose you want to multiply 7 by 8.
Subtract A from 10. Call the result N. Now subtract N from 5 and call the result X.	$10 - 7 = 3$. $5 - 3 = 2$.
Subtract B from 10. Call the result M. Now subtract M from 5 and call the result Y.	$10 - 8 = 2$. $5 - 2 = 3$.
Put down X fingers of one hand and Y fingers of the other hand.	Put down 2 fingers of one hand and 3 fingers of the other.
Add the total number of fingers that you put down to get the number in the tens' place. Multiply the number of fingers that you didn't put down of one hand by the number of fingers that you didn't put down of the other to get the number in the ones' place.	$3 + 2 = 5$. $2 \times 3 = 6$. 56 is the answer.

Actually, that was a somewhat stripped-down model of the Wallachian system, which lets you multiply any two numbers greater than five together. (Presumably, you either memorized the multiplication tables up through the fives or else you could quickly reduce multiplication problems involving numbers no greater than five to a small number of addition problems that you could solve in your head.) If that still seems like a lot of work, here's an even simpler method of finger calculation that works only for multiplying single-digit numbers by 9. Place your hands in front of you, palms down. Starting with your left-hand pinkie, assign all ten fingers the numbers 1 through 10 in order, left to right.

If you lower the finger corresponding to the number you want to multiply by 9, the number of fingers on either side represent the first and second digits of the answer. So for 9×7, lower the index finger of the right hand, leaving all five fingers of the left hand plus the thumb of the right for the first digit (6) and the third, fourth, and fifth fingers on the right hand (3) for an answer of 63. This is related to the *Rule of Nine* described in the preceding chapter: The method works because 9 is one less than our base. (Tom Lehrer's eight-fingered calculator could do this in base 8 for multiples of 7.)

Finger calculation is not confined to the West: A Korean method called *Chisanbop* is taught to schoolchildren today. Chisanbop is done on a tabletop with the palms of both hands down, and the fingertips either touching or not touching the table; right-hand fingers are units and the thumb is 5, whereas the left-hand fingers are 10's and the thumb represents 50.

Chisanbop calculations are performed much as one might work an abacus. Put another way, each row of an abacus is a symbolic representation of a human hand. The advantage of Chisanbop and the abacus over the Roman method of finger calculation is that the former methods can be performed very, very rapidly. In a famous contest between an American high-speed mechanical calculator of the late 1940s and several Japanese clerks with abaci, the Japanese nearly always beat the machine—and, unlike John Henry, lived to enjoy their dinners afterward.

In the West, the search for a mechanical calculator has produced a number of interesting devices along the way: Blaise Pascal's 1642 "arithmetic engine," which did sums using an arrangement of gears not unlike today's car odometer; Gottfried Wilhelm von Leibniz's "stepped reckoner" of 1694, which could also do multiplication; Charles Babbage's 1822 "difference engine," which facilitated calculations for navigation and gunnery; and Herman Hollerith's punch-card-reading tab machine—a precursor to which was the punched-paper warp control, originating among French weavers in the early 1700s and perfected in 1801 by Joseph-Marie Jacquard.

John Napier, a Scot, came up with mechanical devices for rapid multiplication—called "Napier's bones"—but he is more famous for another invention, or rather for the concept behind it, for around 1600 he invented *logarithms* (a Latinate coinage from the Greek spare parts *log(os)* in its specialized sense of 'proportion, ratio' plus *arithmos* 'number'). The logarithm of a number n to the base 10 is the exponent of 10 that would yield n (or to put it formally, if $x = \log_{10} n$, $10^x = n$. Base 10 logarithms are the normal ones in the appendix of one's Algebra I textbook—nowadays, you can press the log 10 key on your electronic calculator.

The nice thing about logarithms is that if you add the logs of two numbers, the sum is the logarithm of their product ($10^{x+y} = 10^x \times 10^y$). One immediate consequence of this—missed by Napier but picked up on by another British mathematician some sixty years later—is that you can build a slide rule, marked off with logarithmic scales instead of linear ones. As a result, at schools in the middle of this century it was easy to spot the science and math majors: They were the nerdy-looking ones with the enormous slip-sticks in holsters attached to their thighs. A cartoon of the late 1950s joked that "an engineer feels positively naked without his slide rule;" the wonk in the picture was wearing nothing else.

But in the 1970s pocket calculators became plentiful and cheap. Almost overnight, slide rules became rarer than streetcars; and now a whole generation has grown up and graduated from college without seeing either one, the sort of rapid technological advance that makes one feel old before one's time. Another "overnight" development— the replacement of sexagesimal fractions with decimal fractions— occurred in 1585 with the publication of Simon Stevin's pamphlet *De Thiende* and its French translation, *La Disme*.

The notion that all fractions should be represented in tenths, hundredths, and thousandths had actually been put forward in 1579 by the French mathematician François Viète—and there is some evidence to suggest that the Chinese experimented with them in antiquity, and that the Arabs did so as well around the Middle Ages—but it was *La Disme*'s publication that got the word out in French *philosophe* circles. With such a head start, it is perhaps not surprising that the French took to the metric system two hundred years later with so little fuss.

Stevin, who was an engineer, once dropped two slabs of lead of greatly different weight from a height of thirty feet onto a board to learn if they went thud at the same time. If this all sounds familiar, Galileo is usually credited with doing this. Stevin also advocated the adoption of Dutch as a universal language on the grounds that it had thrifty syntax and many one-syllable words.

In *De Thiende*, Stevin's sales pitch for the new system included examples for surveyors, astronomers, mint masters, tapestry makers, tailors, and other merchants. (Article Three of Stevin's appendix treats "Of Computations used in Gauging and the Measuring of all Casks.") Stevin claimed that decimalization would allow calculations to be "performed . . . with as much ease as counter-reckoning." This may seem modest in retrospect, but because the decimal point did not make its appearance until the early 1600s, Stevin resorted to subscripts with circles around them after each digit: 0 for units, 1 for tenths (which he called "primes"), 2 for hundredths (called "seconds"), 3 for thousandths ("thirds"), and so on. So the decimal fraction for the ratio 1⅜, which we would now represent as 1.625, Stevin would write as:

Figure 35

$$1\ⓞ\ 6\ ①\ 2\ ②\ 5\ ③$$

Stevin pointed out that some ratios like ⅓ were irreducible to finite decimal expressions: Such a fraction, he said, would yield "infinitely many threes, always with one third in addition." But he also advocated rounding off, arguing that "approximation is more useful than perfection." He knew in any case that an infinite series can have a finite sum.

Take ⅓, which for our demonstration we'll call fraction F. In decimal notation, F is equal to 0.33333. . . . Multiply F by ten and it becomes 3.33333 . . .; and if you multiply it by 100 it becomes 33.33333. . . . Now subtract 10F from 100F:

$$
\begin{aligned}
F &= 0.33333\ldots \\
100F &= 33.33333\ldots \\
-10F &= -3.33333\ldots \\
\hline
90F &= 30.00000\ldots \\
\\
F &= \tfrac{1}{3} \\
\tfrac{1}{3} &= 0.333333\ldots
\end{aligned}
$$

and poof! the repeating, infinite decimal yields a simple fraction, a case in point of an infinite series having a finite sum.

Stevin certainly didn't invent decimal fractions, but he gets credit for their rapid acceptance because his little pamphlet opened the floodgates. (Contrast this with the truly out-of-nowhere contributions of twenty-one-year-old Evariste Galois, who, in a genuine overnight performance, burned the midnight oil frantically sketching out a new branch of mathematics—subsequently known, appropriately enough, as "Galois Theory"—with the full expectation that he would die in a foolish duel the next morning, May 30, 1832. History is frustrated about the early death of the passionate Galois, but grateful that he spent his last hours jotting down what he could of his investigations. Then again, history hasn't bothered to consider what effect forty winks might have had on the steadiness of the young duelist's hand.)

General acceptance of decimal fractions was bound to happen anyway, because we can't avoid seeing fives and tens whenever we look at our hands. The decimal scale comes into play as a folk emblem for any quasi-quantitative measurement, whether the rule for spacing the units is linear, exponential/logarithmic, or simply elastic: "She's a perfect ten"; "I'd give that movie about a four." Usually the higher the score the better, as on a school examination. (In France, exams are customarily graded not 1-to-10 but 1-to-20, once again reminding us how close beneath the façade of metric French rationalism lies old Gallic vigesimalism.) "Cloud 9" is tops in a 1-to-10 height scale displaced by one notch to make 0 the origin; "I was on Cloud 0" would presumably mean "I was stumbling around in a ground-level fog."

On some scales, however, 1 means 'best.' *Ichi-ban* means 'number one in rank, tops' in Japanese; in Germany, a 1 is the best you can do on an exam while a 6 is the pits. On the Richter scale, 10 is as bad as an earthquake can get (which, because the scale is logarithmic, is very bad indeed). And if I lay you odds of ten to one, I am presuming as sure a shot as one could bet on, figuratively staking my just-about-everything against your nearly nothing. In a kinder, gentler time, one might equally well have bet *dollars to donuts;*

since their ratio has fallen to 2:1 or less, the metaphor has lost most of its punch.

Let's talk about "10-codes," the beloved of citizens' band users and the police. Some of these codes are understood just about everywhere in the United States, e.g. 10-4 for 'acknowledgment.' Others vary from one jurisdiction to another: In Shippensburg, Pennsylvania, 10-45 means 'automobile collision'; elsewhere in the same commonwealth it stands for 'carcass of an unlucky beast' (a.k.a. roadkill). But in Portland, Maine, a motor vehicle accident is a 10-55 and 10-45 is reserved for 'domestic disturbance'—as opposed to 'mentally disturbed person' (10-44), 'civil disturbance' (10-70), or 'disturbance/person bothering' (10-95).

One problem with 10-code lists is that the bigger they are, the harder they are to memorize; one dispatcher of our acquaintance, new to the job, dutifully broadcast a string of 10-codes, only to be interrupted by a harried officer who begged her to "talk plain English, f'Gawdsake!" The cop in the cruiser in many a township might well agree: Portland's 10-code list has no fewer than one hundred items, an impressive tally (perhaps deliberately so) for a small, relatively quiet city. Oddly enough, none of these mentions narcotics (though there's 10-43 for 'intoxicated subject'), suggesting that the so-called "War on Drugs" isn't all it's cracked up to be. But this apparent deficiency is more than made up by such items as 'indecent exposure' (10-84), 'dog-deer complaint' (10-64— not to be confused with 'dog complaint' per se, a 10-42), 'snowmobile' (10-66), 'miscellaneous services' (10-69), and 'lunch' (10-10).

ELEVEN

Seven come eleven, baby needs new shoes!

—CRAPS-PLAYER'S CHANT

For in the sterres, clerer than is glas,
Is writen, God woot, whoso koude it rede,
The deeth of every man.

—CHAUCER

ASTROLOGY, THE MUCH-MALIGNED pastime of contemporary star-
gazers, once enjoyed a hardy reputation as a legitimate science pursued by learned men. Thirteenth-century physicians cast horoscopes
as an aid to diagnosis—extending their already considerable list of
talents (alchemy, botany, anatomy) to include astronomy, timekeeping, and a facility with computation. As late as the eighteenth
century (four centuries after Chaucer's birth), mathematicians found
it within their dignity to study astrology seriously.

Witness the case of Girolamo Cardano (1501–1576), whose learning in algebra was exceeded only by his crackpottery and charlatanry.
He claimed the power to cure consumption, and mendaciously ac-
cepted credit for expelling the malady from Archbishop Hamilton of
St. Andrews, who never had the disease in the first place. He drew up
a horoscope for King Edward VI, who rudely refuted Cardano's undoubtedly favorable prognostication by perishing a year later.

Cardano also charted the stars of the long-dead Martin Luther, whom he despised—so he unscrupulously changed his birthday to assure a negative horoscope. He cast a horoscope for Jesus Christ as well—a Capricorn, we reckon.

In between all this, Cardano managed to occupy a professorship of medicine at Padua, publish two widely read books on natural science, and another, *Ars Magna,* about the algebra of the time. It includes the first clear exposition of negative numbers. He also had time to gamble fervidly, which led him to write *Liber de Ludo Aleae* (The Book of Dice Games), an excursion into a more rigorous style of prognostication, probability theory. Unfortunately, it was not published until he was eighty-seven years in the grave. That's too bad, because after Cardano, few people thought seriously about probability until 1654.

Historically, games involving dice attracted few mathematicians, but many assiduous gamblers with a little calculating skill. And why not? The number of possible throws is usually circumscribed by a small number of dice, each with a small number of faces, so the player who cares to do so can calculate the odds on the outcome of a given game without having to be a math whiz (though, of course, being a math whiz affords you the possibility of working out the probabilities by the simple expedient of chugging through a few formulas instead of having to observe and tally the outcomes of a large number of individual games); the odds of your winning at one or another of the conventional games of dice tend to be better than the odds of your hitting the winning lottery number; and, of course, your win or loss is immediate—the professional gambler is not generally interested in waiting around until tomorrow to see if he won or lost.

For modern-day Americans, *craps* is the game of dice par excellence. Played with two six-sided dice, craps seems to have been imported from France to New Orleans around 1800. According to one etymologist, the word *craps* was originally *crabs,* the name of the unlucky throw of 2 or 3 in the dice game of *hazard.* (*Crabs* is attested in this sense in English as early as 1768.) But another suggested derivation is that the game of hazard, hitherto unknown in the Western Hemisphere, was introduced in modified form by a professional gambler named Bernard Marigny, whose Creole alias was Johnny Crapaud; hence it was called "Johnny Crapaud's game," shortened to "crap game" over time. (*Crapaud* is French for 'toad.' The heraldic emblem of King Clovis of the Franks was three black toads until he—or a holy hermit, in another version of the story—had a vision in which the amphibians were metamorphosed into three gold lilies, whence came the *fleur-de-lis* on France's royal coat of arms.)

The scoring in craps works as follows: A 7 or an 11 on the first roll of the dice is a *natural*—an immediate winning throw for the roller, the origin of the gambler's fervent "Seven come eleven, baby needs new shoes!" But *crapping out*—an initial throw of a two and a one, two sixes ("boxcars"), or two ones ("snake eyes") means an immediate loss. (A fancier term for double ones is *ambsace*—from Latin *ambō* 'both' + *as* 'unit,' the *as* having been the lowest-denomination Roman coin, whence also came the name for the one-spot card, the *ace*.) Otherwise, the player continues rolling, the object of the game being to repeat the initial throw before rolling a 7. Later, *crapping out* came to mean 'to break down, cease to work'—as in "my car crapped out at 175,000 miles," probably reinforced by the other meaning of *crap*—'excrement.'

The crapshooter's chances of winning (when on a roll) work out to a little less than 50/50 (0.493951, to be precise, there being 496 possible outcomes of the game, 245 of which favor the roller). This is a little better than the roller's odds (0.490823) in the older and slightly more complex game of *hazard,* which takes its name, ultimately, from Arabic *azzar* '(the) die,' whence came the other meanings associated with the term—'chance, luck, risk, peril'—and which, like craps, is played with two six-sided dice. The rules are as follows: The thrower rolls the dice until he throws a 5, 6, 7, 8, or 9. This is termed the *main point*. The thrower then rolls to determine the *chance point*. If the thrower rolls a 2 or a 3, or if he rolls an 11 and the main point is 5, 6, 8, or 9, or if he rolls a 12 and the main point is 5, 7, or 9, he loses. However, if he rolls the main point, he rolls an 11 and the main point is 7, or he rolls a 12 and the main point is 6 or 8, he wins. If the thrower doesn't win or lose outright on the first two tosses, he continues to roll until he rolls the chance point (in which case, he wins) or the main point (in which case, he loses).

If the task of calculating the odds in hazard seems daunting, imagine working out the possibilities for a variant of the game, like *zara,* which was played with three six-sided dice instead of two, presumably by gamblers on the fast track, those on the slower track contenting themselves with games involving fewer dice or dice with fewer than six faces. Both of these tracks were well known among the Greeks and Romans who each had separate terms for six-sided and four-sided dice.

Romans called a die that was marked on four faces a *tālus,* literally, 'anklebone,' for which the corresponding Greek term was *astragalos*—talus and *astragalus* are used more or less interchangeably in Modern Medicalese to designate the anklebone, i.e., the bone that forms the joint between the tibia and fibula. This bone (by whichever name) was deemed ideal for gaming since it is roughly a rectangular solid, which when thrown will come up unambiguously on one face. Moreover, it has no marrow, so loose ones from sheep are more likely to be lying around after the wolves have gotten done than, say, thighbones. The first known use of *astragalī* in gaming dates to Egypt's First Dynasty, about 3500 B.C. An 1800 B.C. "Hounds and Jackals" game, found in the tomb of Reny-Soube at Thebes, has counters like cribbage pegs with heads of the two animals carved on them, to be advanced on the board according to the throw of three astragali. The maker of the board also thoughtfully included a little drawer to keep the pegs and dice in.

Astragali also seem to have played an essential role in early versions of the children's game nowadays known in Britain as *knucklebones,* in France as *osselets* (literally, 'little, little bones'), and in America, as *jacks* (a shortening of *jackstones,* a transmogrification of *chuckstones,* i.e., stones that you chuck or throw), which involves tossing and catching a handful of playing pieces and then tossing and nimbly scooping them up in various combinations: In the *Iliad,* Homer relates Achilles's dream in which Patroclus recalls, as a child, killing a playmate over a game of knucklebones (*astragaloi*), which is generally assumed to have been jacks rather than craps. Homer doesn't actually say one way or the other, so we have to balance our cultural biases that tell us that jacks is a children's game and craps is an adult game. The fact that "Roll those bones" is a craps-players' expression is probably neither here nor there.

Herodotus tells us that the Greeks of Lydia, during a time of famine, resolved to eat only every other day, and invented various games involving astragali (including either dice or jacks, though which of the two is not quite clear) to play on the day of fasting in order to divert their minds from hunger. However fabulous this story, it is certain that games with astragali were played in ancient Anatolia: Archaeologists have excavated a thirteenth-century B.C. wineshop, containing pottery, wine vats, and the skeletons of hapless topers, as well as a pile of astragali near the door (together with a stack of crescent-shaped game counters or tokens, familiar from previous digs but hitherto thought to be loom weights).

The astragalus has two faces that are rounded, so that an astragalus in effect has only four faces to work with; the Romans assigned these the numbers 1, 3, 4, and 6, omitting 2 and 5. The probabilities of each face coming up on a throw are not equal; with a sheep's astragalus, the side faces (classically assigned the numbers 1 and 6) each have roughly a 1:10 chance, but the top and bottom faces (3 and 4) are closer to 4:10. The Romans threw four astragali at a time; they thought the luckiest throw the one called "Venus," in which all four faces were different. In fact, a throw of four 1's (the Romans called 1 "the Dog," as had the Greeks before them) is less likely, but the fit between probability and what a given society calls lucky is not always snug.

True dice—polyhedra marked with pips on the faces—seem to have been in use nearly as long as astragali, and have the advantage of appearing to give an equal chance to each number represented. Presumably, the first dice came from filing down the two round faces of an astragalus. From there, it was a short step to artificial pottery dice, known in Mesopotamia, Egypt, and India. The Greeks called the six-sided die a *kybos,* the basis of the English word *cube.* For a six-sided die, the Romans used the term *tessera* and its variant *tes-*

sela (from the Greek word for 'four'), referring, presumably, to the four edges of each face.

Nor did the Romans stop at six sides, witness the Roman rock-crystal icosahedron in the Louvre, with both a Roman numeral and a letter on each face. The Romans were also familiar with faked dice: Some simply had numbers left out and others duplicated, and at least one Roman author mentions loaded dice—a die with hollow space behind the face of the 1 in which to insert a weight. But this is hardly surprising, as the Romans were inordinately fond of dice, evidenced by their use of the term *ālea* to mean not only 'game of chance, gambling, risk, gamble' but 'die' as well, as in *"Iacta ālea est!"* ('The die is cast!'), which is what Julius Caesar is said to have remarked on crossing the Rubicon, meaning that he had placed his bet and the rest was up to chance. The pot in this case was no less than the Roman state, since bringing an army into Italy proper without the Roman Senate's consent was a de facto declaration of civil war.

It is from *ālea* that English gets the word *aleatory,* literally, 'dicey,' hence, by extension, 'generated by a random method such as the throw of a die,' as in *aleatory music*. The English terms *die* and *dice*—which preserves the original pronunciation of the plural ending also found in *pence*—come via Old French from Late Latin *datum* 'playing piece, die' literally, 'that which is played' from the verb *dare* 'to give, play.'

Passion for dice continued undampened past the fall of the Roman Empire into the Middle Ages—a bishop of the time remarked sourly that just as God had created twenty-one letters of the (Roman) alphabet, so the Devil had created the twenty-one pips (1 + 2 + 3 + 4 + 5 + 6) on a die. During the Renaissance, no less a light than Galileo felt called upon to publish a paper (*Sopra le scoperte di dadi,* loosely, On the Ways Dice Come Up) in which he showed why you have a better chance of throwing a 10 than a 9 with three conventional dice (even though you can make 10 and 9 with the same number of combinations of the numbers from 1 to 6 taken three at a time), which brings us by a comodius vicus of recirculation to the year 1654, the birth of probability theory, during the age of the great French mathematicians Pierre Fermat and Blaise Pascal.

It was dice-playing—and the question of the probability of throwing two 6's—that prompted Antoine Gombaud, Chevalier de Méré, to ask Pascal to do the math that would eventually result in the emergence of probability theory: When tossing a pair of dice, how many tosses should the player expect to make before rolling double 6? With only one toss, the player should not expect a double 6, because there are thirty-five other equally likely possible outcomes. If the player perseveres and is willing to toss the dice many times, he can reasonably expect to see double 6 eventually. What is the minimum number of tosses the player can plan to make, and still be sure that the odds of rolling at least one double 6 exceeds the odds of failing to roll a double 6?

Through faulty reasoning, de Méré had calculated the minimum number of tosses at twenty-four, but experienced gamblers knew that more often than not, twenty-four tosses failed to yield double 6. He asked Pascal why.

With Fermat, Pascal solved the problem. In two throws, the number of possible outcomes is thirty-six (6×6) of which thirty-five don't produce a double 6, so the probability of failing to produce a double 6 with one throw is 35/36. The probability of failing with two throws is $(35/36)^2$, and the odds of failing in n throws is $(35/36)^n$. When n is less than 24, $(35/36)^n$ exceeds ½; you'll lose more than half the time. But when n is 25 or higher, $(35/36)^n$ is less than ½; you'll lose less than half the time. That is, if you plan to toss the dice fewer than twenty-five times, the odds are that you'll fail, and you shouldn't expect to win unless you're willing to toss the dice twenty-five times or more.

De Méré's problem inspired a brisk and fertile correspondence between Pascal and Fermat, whose result was a theory of probability. During that same year, Pascal showed Fermat a copy of his *Traité du triangle arithmétique* (Treatise Concerning the Arithmetical Triangle), a systematic study of what is now known as Pascal's triangle. It would turn out to be Pascal's last significant work in mathematics before he had a vision of God and withdrew from the world of science, which delayed the treatise's publication for eleven years.

Pascal didn't invent the array of numbers that constitute Pascal's triangle, each of which is the sum of the two numbers diagonally adjacent and above it on either side. It was known to mathematicians in China, possibly as early as A.D. 1050. The Persian poet Omar Khayyám, who lived from about A.D. 1050 to 1130, alluded to the arithmetic triangle in his book *On Demonstrations of Problems of Algebra and Almucabola*. And in Europe, Petrus Apianus's *Rechnung* had put the triangle in print by 1527.

The triangle is filled with remarkable properties, one of which involves the number eleven. The triangle's first five rows (Pascal called them *bases*, because they form the bases of successively larger triangles) contain the digits of the first five powers of eleven: $11^0 = 1$; $11^1 = 11$; $11^2 = 121$; $11^3 = 1,331$; $11^4 = 14,641$. What's more,

Figure 36

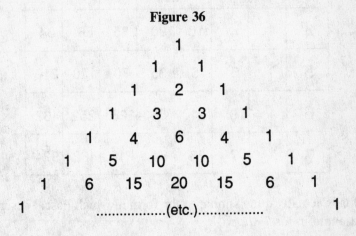

if you interpret these digits in a different number system (like octal) they spell out the successive powers of other numbers. For example, in any number system except binary, the square of the number written as "11" is the number written as "121." The decimal equation "$9^2 = 81$" has an octal equivalent: "$11^2 = 121$."

If you have a personal computer and the appropriate software, you can very easily create a rectangular version of Pascal's triangle as an electronic spreadsheet. For example, to create a 7 × 7 version of

Pascal's triangle in Lotus 1-2-3, starting in cell A1, you would enter a 1 in cells A1 through G1 and A2 through A7. Next, in cell B2, you would enter the formula $+A2+B1$. You would then copy the contents of B2 to the range of cells extending from B2 to G7:

Figure 37: Pascal's Triangle (The Spreadsheet)

	A	B	C	D	E	F	G
1	1	1	1	1	1	1	1
2	1	2	3	4	5	6	7
3	1	3	6	10	15	21	28
4	1	4	10	20	35	56	84
5	1	5	15	35	70	126	210
6	1	6	21	56	126	252	462
7	1	7	28	84	210	462	924

This is actually quite similar to the form in which Pascal describes the triangle in his *Traité*:

Figure 38: Pascal's Triangle (The Classic)

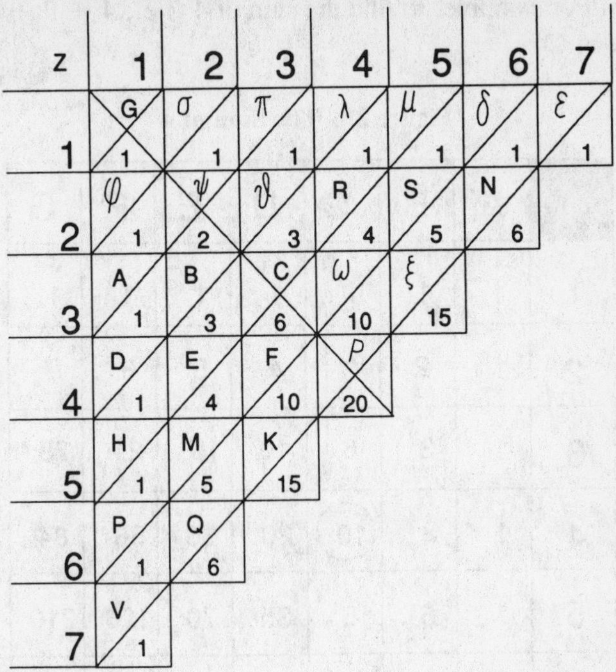

Z	1	2	3	4	5	6	7
1	G 1	σ 1	π 1	λ 1	μ 1	δ 1	ε 1
2	φ 1	ψ 2	ϑ 3	R 4	S 5	N 6	
3	A 1	B 3	C 6	ω 10	ξ 15		
4	D 1	E 4	F 10	P 20			
5	H 1	M 5	K 15				
6	P 1	Q 6					
7	V 1						

Had there been such a thing as electronic spreadsheets in Pascal's day, he might have described the properties of the triangle that he identifies in the *Traité* as follows:

- The natural number sequence (1, 2, 3, 4, 5, 6, . . .) shows up in column B and in row 2.
- A set of numbers that Pascal was at a loss to name (but which today might be called the *n-dimensional hyper-tetrahedral numbers*) show up in succeeding columns/rows: The natural numbers in column B (row 2), triangular numbers (1, 3, 6, 10, 15, 21, . . .) in Column C (row 3), the tetrahedral numbers (1, 4, 10, 20, 35, 56, . . .) in column D (row 4), and so on, the number in any given cell n being the sum of the numbers in cells 1 through n in the column to the immediate left.
- To find the sum of n (1 + 2 + . . . + n), look in the nth cell

of column C—this is a particular case of the preceding bullet item. For example, to find the sum of 4 (i.e., $4 + 3 + 2 + 1$), look in C4:

Figure 39: The Sum of 4

	A	B	C	D	E	F	G
1	1	1	1	1	1	1	1
2	1	2	3	4	5	6	7
3	1	3	6	10	15	21	28
4	1	4	(10)	20	35	56	84
5	1	5	15	35	70	126	210
6	1	6	21	56	126	252	462
7	1	7	28	84	210	462	924

· To find the nth power of 2, add the contents of the cells that form the base of the triangle whose apex is A1 and whose row and column legs are $n + 1$ cells long (because n could be 0). For example, to find 2^4, add the contents of cells A5, B4, C3, D2, and E1:

Figure 40: Two to the Fourth

	A	B	C	D	E	F	G
1	1	1	1	1	(1)	1	1
2	1	2	3	(4)	5	6	7
3	1	3	(6)	10	15	21	28
4	1	(4)	10	20	35	56	84
5	(1)	5	15	35	70	126	210
6	1	6	21	56	126	252	462
7	1	7	28	84	210	462	924

- To find the square of n, add the contents of cells Cn and Cn-1 together. For example, to find 7^2, add the contents of C7 and C6:

Figure 41: Seven Squared

	A	B	C	D	E	F	G
1	1	1	1	1	1	1	1
2	1	2	3	4	5	6	7
3	1	3	6	10	15	21	28
4	1	4	10	20	35	56	84
5	1	5	15	35	70	126	210
6	1	6	(21)	56	126	252	462
7	1	7	(28)	84	210	462	924

Pascal prefaces his remarks on the triangle by saying that it has all sorts of properties of which he is only going to mention the principal ones. There are many others he did not mention.

For example, hidden in the triangle is the sequence of Catalan numbers (1, 1, 2, 5, 14, 42, . . .) which can be teased out without too much effort. To find the nth Catalan number, go to the intersection of the nth row and the nth column and subtract from its contents the contents of the cell one cell over and one cell up (if any):

Figure 42: The Catalan Numbers

	A	B	C	D	E	F	G
1	1	1	1	1	1	1	1
2	1	2	3	4	5	6	7
3	1	3	6	10	15	21	28
4	1	4	10	20	35	56	84
5	1	5	15	35	70	126	210
6	1	6	21	56	126	252	462
7	1	7	28	84	210	462	924

1
1
2
5
14
42

The Fibonacci numbers (1, 1, 2, 3, 5, 8, 13, . . .) also lurk in the triangle. Cell A1 contains the first Fibonacci number, and A2 contains the second. To derive the nth Fibonacci number beyond the second, go to the nth cell in column A, and move like a knight in chess (over one and up two), until you land on a cell in row 2 or row 1. The nth Fibonacci number is the sum of the contents of all the cells you landed on, including An, where you started:

Figure 43: The Fibonacci Numbers

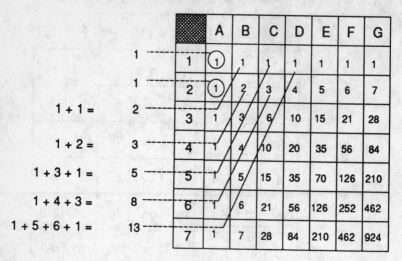

The triangle also lets you determine your chances of winning the kind of lottery in which you pick k numbers from a set of n in the hope that they will be matched by the ones that come up at the drawing. For example, if the lottery lets you pick four numbers ($k = 4$) between 1 and 6 ($n = 6$), you pick 1, 2, 3, and 4, and the drawing produces the numbers 1, 2, 3, 4 or 2, 4, 3, 1, or some other permutation of those numbers, you win. However, if the winning numbers are, say, 1, 2, 3, 6 (or 2, 6, 1, 3, or some other permutation of *those* numbers), you lose. (State-run lotteries tend to pay something less than the jackpot if you pick some but not all of the winning numbers, but the range of numbers—the n—from which you have to pick your hopefuls—the k—tends to be rather large, so they are not really doing you any favors.)

To use Pascal's triangle to figure your odds of winning such a lottery, simply find the base of the triangle containing $n + 1$ numbers. (On a spreadsheet, the base of the triangle stretches along the diagonal between cell A$n + 1$ and the $n + 1$th cell of row 1.) Skip over the first k numbers along that base and read the next number: You have one chance in that number of winning. For example, if the lottery game lets you choose any four numbers from one through six, there are fifteen different possible combinations, because 15 is the fifth number of the applicable base of Pascal's triangle—1, 6, 15, 20, 15, 6, 1—which means that you have a one in fifteen chance of winning.

Figure 44: Figuring the Odds

	A	B	C	D	E	F	G
1	1	1	1	1	1	1	1
2	1	2	3	4	5	6	7
3	1	3	6	10	15	21	28
4	1	4	10	20	35	56	84
5	1	5	15	35	70	126	210
6	1	6	21	56	126	252	462
7	1	7	28	84	210	462	924

Actually, the gambling problem that really interested Pascal before he turned his attention to the ultimate gambling problem, the Divine Wager (which centers on the question of what you stand to win or lose if you do or do not believe in God), was not the one posed by de Méré but, rather, one known as "the problem of points," the focus of a substantial section of the *Traité* whose title might be loosely rendered "Use of the Arithmetical Triangle to Determine How to Split the Pot Between Two Players Playing the Best *M* out of *N* Games" to which may be added, by way of clarification, "When They Agree to Stop Playing and Divide the Pot Before Either Has Won *M* Games."

Pascal did not say what sort of game he had in mind when he attacked the problem of points, only that it involved a pot, an agreement on the part of the players that they would play until one or the other of them had won some specified number of rounds of play, and that it was winner-take-all. It was probably some kind of dice game and certainly not baseball, which hadn't been invented yet, though if it had, he might have renamed the problem "The World Series Problem" and illustrated it as follows:

On October 17, 1989, a severe earthquake rocked the San Francisco Bay area, including Candlestick Park, where the Oakland Athletics and San Francisco Giants were preparing for game three of the World Series. Game three and all subsequent games were immediately postponed, and for a while there was talk of canceling the remainder of the series outright.

Suppose it *had* been canceled. (It wasn't—Oakland eventually won it four games to zero.) Oakland had beaten San Francisco in both of the first two games. Assuming that the teams were equally matched, what were the real odds on the rest of the series at that point, and how would the bonus money (which would normally go to the series champion) be divided between the teams?

Pascal says that the first thing we must keep in mind is that in games where the stakes consist of money that players have ponied up in advance, the money no longer belongs to them, being given up to chance; but he adds that the players nevertheless have the right to expect whatever portion of the pot that chance will give them back in accordance with whatever conditions have been agreed upon before the game starts.

The second thing is that in situations where if one partner wins he gets a certain portion of the pot, and if he loses the other player gets it—and it really is a game of chance—and they decide to quit while they are tied, they should each get half of the portion in question, since each would have had a 50/50 chance at the whole pot had they gone ahead and played the tie-breaking game.

Splitting the difference down the middle would have been the equitable solution if the earthquake had come just as the seventh game of the World Series was about to begin, i.e., when each team had won three games and were about to play the tiebreaker. But what if it were game six, and one team (say, San Francisco) still had to win two games to take the series, while the other team (Oakland) only had to win this one for the best four out of seven?

The possible outcomes of this situation would be:

1. Oakland wins game six.
2. San Francisco wins game six, then Oakland wins game seven.
3. San Francisco wins game six and game seven.

Using the following reasoning, Pascal would argue that if the Series is canceled before game six while Oakland leads 3 games to 2, Oakland should get three-fourths of the bonus and San Francisco should get one-fourth: All things being equal, the probability that San Francisco would win game six is one out of two, or, 1/2. Only after winning game six would San Francisco then have a 1/2 chance of winning the series (since either team would have a 1/2 chance of winning the tie-breaking game seven); to calculate the probability that San Francisco could take the Series, multiply the probability of their winning game six (1/2) by the probability of their then winning game seven (1/2), namely: 1/4, so they should get a quarter of the bonus while Oakland should get the rest, that is, three-quarters.

Pascal figured out how to read the solution to the problem of points directly from the triangle, using a variation of the method used to calculate the odds of winning the lottery that we described earlier:

1. Add the number of games each team yet needs to win the Series. (After the earthquake, San Francisco needed to win four games, Oakland, two; so the desired sum is six.)
2. Find the base of the triangle containing that many elements. (The base with six elements is 1, 5, 10, 10, 5, 1.)
3. Starting from the left, add as many elements as the number of games the trailing team needs yet to win. (The trailing team needs to win four games, so add the first four numbers: $1 + 5 + 10 + 10 = 26$.)
4. Add up the other numbers. (There are two remaining numbers: $5 + 1 = 6$.)

Figure 45: Figuring the Odds Once More

	A	B	C	D	E	F	G
1	1	1	1	1	1	1	1
2	1	2	3	4	5	6	7
3	1	3	6	10	15	21	28
4	1	4	10	20	35	56	84
5	1	5	15	35	70	126	210
6	1	6	21	56	126	252	462
7	1	7	28	84	210	462	924

5. The two sums show the ratio in which the stakes are divided.
   (Oakland gets 26/32 of the stakes, and San Francisco gets 6/32
   of the stakes.)

Is there something wrong with this picture? Do you have the
nagging feeling that if San Francisco needed four games to win the
Series and Oakland needed only two that they should have split
the bonus in thirds, one-third for San Francisco and two-thirds for
Oakland? Well, rigorous application of the rules of probability can
often yield correct but counterintuitive results. A classic example is
the three-door problem, which goes like this:

On the quiz show, you are shown three doors. The emcee tells you
that behind one door is a briefcase with sixty-four thousand dollars
cash in it, but behind each of the other two is a shopping bag full of
guano. You are asked to choose a door, with the understanding that
the host will thereupon open one of the doors you didn't pick.

When the host opens one of the two doors you didn't pick, there's no briefcase, just one of the blivets. Now you are asked if you'd like to switch your choice from the door you picked to the other still-closed door. What should you do?

Answer: You should switch. Suppose you choose door #1. Originally, each door has a 1/3 chance of being the door with the money. The opening of a nonwinning door—say #2—now means that the remaining door (#3) now has a 2/3 chance of being the right one, *because the host will always open a losing door on purpose.* If the prize is behind door #2, the host will open door #3; if the prize were behind #3, the host would have opened #2. So when you switch, you win if the prize is behind *either* #2 or #3; if you stay with #1, you win only if the prize is behind #1!

Another argument: By picking a door, you split the prizes in two—the one you picked and those you didn't. Those you didn't choose have a 2/3 chance of including the money, and a *100 percent* chance of including some guano. When the host reveals guano, he teaches you nothing worthwhile; you already knew at least some guano was included in the prizes you rejected. With no new information, the odds are unchanged, and the odds that your first choice missed the money remain 2/3. You should switch.

Syndicated newspaper columnist Marilyn Vos Savant got thousands of incredulous letters when she published this hoary old classic in the Sunday supplement *Parade* early in 1991. Defending her solution in a subsequent column, she suggested that any two people who wanted to test it could take a die, a penny, and three paper cups, numbered 1, 2, and 3. While one person looked away, the other would throw the die until it turned up a 1, 2, or 3, and determine which cup to put the penny under. Then the other person would choose, and the first person uncover one of the nonwinning cups. In the first set of trials, the second person would change cups, but in a second, equal number of trials that person would stand pat with the original choice. A running log showing the actual success rate of the two strategies will show that the odds truly are doubled by switching—not a deductive proof, to be sure, but a demonstration whose empirical evidence rudely unhorses our common sense.

TWELVE

TWELVE IS AS HIGH as you could count on the fingers of both hands if you were born with hexadactylism—six-digitedness, a genetically dominant, though relatively rare trait in humans. Twelve can be represented as an array of three by four, such as the stones that the Old Testament says were to be set on the High Priest's breastplate, a different gem for each tribe of Israel; Jesus probably deliberately echoed this in calling twelve disciples. There are twelve signs to the zodiac and twelve months to the year. We refer to something common as "a dime a dozen," that is, less than a penny apiece—or a penny apiece with two left over. The word *twelve,* in fact, derives from a Germanic compound meaning "two left," i.e., two left over beyond ten, a tip of the hat to the relative incommensurability of decimal and duodecimal systems—the word *dozen* comes from French *douzaine* 'a collection of twelve,' itself from the word for 'twelve'—*douze*—plus the suffix *-aine* 'group of, collection of however many.'

Twelve also happens to be the smallest *abundant number*, or number whose proper divisors, or "aliquot parts," add up to more than the number itself, a *proper divisor* (or *aliquot part*) being a whole number by which you can evenly divide a given larger whole number. Thus, twelve's aliquot parts are 1, 2, 3, 4, and 6, which add up to 16. *Aliquot*, by the way, comes from Latin *aliquot* 'some, several' (from *alius,* 'other' plus *quot* 'how many, so many').

Abundant itself literally means 'overflowing,' from Latin *unda* ('wave'). Pythagoras and his followers called such numbers "super (excessively) perfect" (*hyperteleios*). That which is *teleios* has reached its limit or end and is therefore complete, so that which is *hyperteleios* has surpassed its limit, overflowing its boundaries so to speak—Greek *telos* ('limit, end'), from which *teleios* is derived, gives the *tel-* of *teleology* (the study of ends or purposes) and is related to the *palin-* of *palindrome* and the *col-* of English *collar* (the idea in both cases being, presumably, that the end and the beginning are the same). A plain *teleois* (or "perfect") number, for the Pythagoreans, was one whose aliquot parts added up exactly to that number. For example, 6's aliquot parts (1, 2, and 3) add up to 6. The first three perfect numbers are 6, 28, and 496, the only three less than 1,000.

By contrast, there are 246 abundant numbers between 1 and 1,000—the smallest odd one, curiously, is 945—of which fourteen are very abundant: Their aliquot parts add up to twice the number or more. The Greeks called numbers greater than the sum of their aliquot parts *deficient*—presumably because such numbers lack the proper divisors that the abundant and perfect numbers have.

Amicable numbers are pairs whose aliquot parts add up to each other, e.g., 220 and 284: The sum of 220's aliquot parts (1, 2, 4, 5, 10, 11, 20, 22, 44, 55, and 110) equals 284, the sum of whose aliquot parts (1, 2, 4, 71, and 142) equals 220. For many years, 220 and 284 were the only number pair known to be amicable—Pythagoras is said to have known about the pair's properties. But the name "amicable" wasn't coined until much later in a treatise by the medieval Arab mathematician Ibn Khaldun, who added that "those who occupy themselves with talismans assure that these numbers have a particular influence in establishing union and friendship between two individuals." The second pair of amicable numbers (17,296 and 18,416) was discovered by another Arab mathematician, Ibn Al-Banna, working with a formula for deriving amicable numbers that had been constructed by one Tabit Ibn Qorra in the ninth century A.D. The French mathematician Pierre de Fermat subsequently reinvented Ibn Qorra's formula and used it to derive the second pair during the seventeenth century. So did Descartes, who discovered a third pair of amicable numbers (9,363,584 and 9,437,056) for good measure.

The writer on mathematics Martin Gardner once remarked that it would be hard to find a more totally useless set of whole numbers than the perfect or amicable numbers, an assertion that would be unthinkable to make about the abundant numbers and least of all about the first abundant number: twelve. Since a dozen can be divided in so many ways, it is not surprising that it should be firmly entrenched in the marketplace—when was the last time you bought ten eggs? This may explain why English-speaking schoolchildren learn the multiplication table through twelve, rather than stopping at ten, which would seem the logical thing to do—and as many French schoolchildren actually do, since $(n \times 12)$ is just the same thing as $(n \times 10) + (n \times 2)$, and the French have been on the metric system for two hundred years.

Twelve dozen—144—is a *gross*. Like the English foot, the old French *pied* was divided into twelve inches (*pouces,* literally, 'thumbs'), each a little longer than our modern inch (about 27 millimeters versus 25.4 millimeters). The *pouce* in turn could be subdivided into twelve *lignes* ('lines'), and each *ligne* into twelve *douzièmes* ('twelfths'). *Ligne* and *douzième* survived in the French jewelry trades and are still occasionally used on Philadelphia's Jewelers' Row, though largely supplanted nowadays by measurements in millimeters or thousandths of an inch. As it happens, a *douzième* is very close to .0075 inch, so twelve of them make .09 inch, which happens to be very close to #11 on Brown and Sharpe's gauge, the jewelers' commonest measure for wire diameter.

The making of jewelry and minting of coinage have always gone hand in hand—sometimes literally so, as when Boston silversmith John Hull stamped the Massachusetts "Pine Tree Shilling" in 1680. The system for weighing precious metal used in the French town of Troyes became the Troy standard used throughout the world. There are twenty pennyweight to the Troy ounce (thus 240 of them in the Troy pound), each pennyweight being subdivided into twenty-four grains.

The pound sterling, the British monetary standard since 1527, was originally identical with a twelve-ounce Troy pound of silver, fixed at 92.5 percent pure. Each pound was worth twenty shillings, and each shilling was worth twelve pence. Since the founding of the Bank of England in the 1690s, larger denominations have been issued as paper currency; but British kings starting with Henry VII stamped gold coins worth a pound—sovereigns, so called because they bore the ruler's face on the obverse. These and gold ten-shilling half-sovereigns circulated until the beginning of this century.

In 1663 Charles II complicated matters by striking the first guineas—valued at one pound plus one shilling—from gold imported from Guinea on the African equatorial west coast; these were issued until 1813, George III's 1787 "spade guinea" being so called from the shield on its reverse. Although no gold coins were still circulating when Britain decimalized its currency, "guineas" still survives as a means of snob reckoning, e.g., when talking of expensive tailors and the luxury car trade.

Converting pence into shillings and pounds and back surely made for a lot of pencil chewing and furrowing of the brow, even for fairly simple calculations; indeed, merely writing numbers with three components took a little practice. For example, to add one pound, fourteen shillings, ten pence to three pounds, five shillings, six pence, you had to subtract twelve from the total of sixteen in the pence column and carry one shilling, which, when you added it to the 14 and 5 already in the shillings column, gave you 20 or a pound and no shillings left over, for a total of five pounds, four pence—a decidedly cumbersome operation.

Even before the American Revolution was officially over, it had become obvious that the thirteen colonies would have to standardize their hodgepodge of currencies, and Gouverneur Morris's 1782 proposal made a quarter-grain of silver the basic unit, since this value represented the greatest common divisor of all the colonies' existing pennies. The quarter-grain unit would then be 1,440 to the new dollar and 1,600 to the old five-shilling crown.

Thomas Jefferson, who sat on the congressional committee charged with recommending currency reform, was appalled at the numbers: People were already papering their walls with Continentals, and hardly needed to be further demoralized by paying seventy-two units for a loaf of bread and 288 for a pound of butter! Instead,

Jefferson proposed a strictly decimal currency—essentially the one we have today—along with a decimal system of weights and measures, arguing that a system of even, base-ten increments would greatly simplify day-to-day calculations ordinary people needed to make, "which the present complicated and difficult ratios place beyond their computation for the most part."

Supporters of decimalization in the United States saw the common citizen's ability to calculate—something most colonial Americans, even the college trained, did not do very well—as the prerequisite to commerce, itself the gateway to American prosperity and happiness. "Republican money ought to be simple, and adapted to the meanest capacity," wrote Erastus Root in his 1796 *Introduction to Arithmetic for the Use of Common Schools*. But he disagreed with Jefferson about decimal weights and measures, dismissing France's brand-new metric system and ten-day calendar, like their Republicanism, as too much of a good thing: The French "stretched decimal simplicity beyond its proper limits, even into decadary infidelity."

Not all standardizations that century beat a hasty retreat from the number twelve. Earlier that century, Bach composed *The Well-Tempered Clavier*, twenty-four prelude-and-fugue pairs, one for each of the twelve major keys and one for each of the corresponding minor keys. The first book of *The Well-Tempered Clavier* was enough of a hit that Bach later wrote another set of twenty-four along the same lines. Together, the two books are sometimes simply called "The Great Forty-eight." By spanning all these key signatures, Bach forced the issue of temperament, the slight adjustment of notes to accommodate modulations from one key signature to another without requiring retuning.

Previously, musical instruments were tuned pretty much according to the rules of harmony first articulated by Pythagoras, who noticed that decreasing the length of a vibrating string produced a tone higher than the original full-length string. The Pythagoreans proceeded to identify most of the diatonic scale (roughly what you hear today if you stay in the key of C major and play only the white piano keys). At one-half its original length, the string's tone rises by a full octave. At one-third length, it vibrates at a major fifth above the octave, at one-fifth length, the major third just beyond two octaves above the original tone. These are the same notes a trumpeter or bugler will get by blowing with increased force so as to cause the column of air inside the instrument to oscillate twice as fast, three times as fast . . . five times as fast . . . and so on.

This was fine as long as Western music stuck to the diatonic scale, but once accidentals crept in (the earliest of which, showing up in Gregorian chant, is akin to playing B flat while in the key of C major), it became clear that if you filled all the blanks in, you'd have twelve semitones (half steps) to the octave, and the perfect intervals (like the fifth) calculated by the Pythagoreans were not quite evenly spaced throughout the chromatic (twelve-semitone) scale. If you left the Pythagorean intervals perfect, others would sound really mouldy, and playing a given melody in a different key could be less than refreshing.

By the end of the seventeenth century it was becoming clear that something had to give. Some vocal writing was fully chromatic (i.e., employing all twelve tones of the scale). Accompanists needed to choose a key to accommodate the vocalist's range. Sliding a melody up or down the frequency range is easy for fretless stringed instruments, but with an organ or harpsichord, what you've tuned is what you get. Only by sacrificing the purity of the Pythagorean natural intervals to equal temperament is it possible for any melody to be played on a keyboard instrument and sound no worse than the same melody played in another key.

Bach retuned his harpsichord proportionally, ensuring that the difference between two adjacent notes was proportionally equivalent to the difference between any other pair of adjacent notes. In this effort he fudged some of the Pythagorean intervals slightly (the Pythagorean fifth oscillates 1.5 times as fast as the tonic, but for a well-tempered fifth the figure is closer to 1.498—a noticeable but acceptable difference), but he produced an instrument tuned to play melodies in all keys equally well. Keyboard instruments are still tuned this way today.

The proportional difference Bach used between adjacent semitones equals the twelfth root of 2, or approximately 1.059.

$$\sqrt[12]{2}$$

Moving up a whole step is equivalent to two consecutive semitone increases, so a whole step increases the frequency of oscillation by the sixth root of 2, an amount equal to the twelfth root of 2 times the twelfth root of 2:

$$\sqrt[12]{2} \times \sqrt[12]{2} = (\sqrt[12]{2})^2 = \sqrt[6]{2}$$

Twelve half steps takes us all the way through the chromatic scale, moving up an entire octave:

$$(\sqrt[12]{2})^{12} = 2$$

Notice that the twelve half steps, as consecutive multiplications by the twelfth root of 2, preserve the whole-number purity of the original Pythagorean octave, exactly doubling the frequency, bringing us back to *do*.

THIRTEEN

"THIRTEEN ARE THE companions of life, and thirteen the companions of death," says Lao-Tzu's classic, the *Tao-te Ching*. Speakers of English know thirteen as the baker's dozen—a charming custom fancifully traced back to the Middle Ages, when English bakers, it is said, bent over backwards to avoid being assessed heavy fines for short-weighting bread. Thirteen is also the quintessential number of bad luck, the only number for the fear of which we have a specific word in English: *triskaidekaphobia*, a Greek compound meaning, literally, 'thirteen fear.'

Thirteen is to the dozen what 11 is to base 10: indivisible by the base's aliquot parts, since there's always a remainder of 1. Thus, where 12 represents the whole (twelve signs of the zodiac, twelve gods of Olympus, twelve hours to the day, twelve days of Christmas, and so on), 13, as odd man out, lies just beyond completeness in a sinister restlessness, something to be avoided even to this day. Witness the number of skyscrapers that have been built without a floor numbered 13, or the tenacity of the notion that it is courting ill fate to seat thirteen people at the same table for dinner, a prohibition (to which the French response has been the invention of the *quatorzième*, or professional hired fourteenth guest) as old as Western folklore: Loki the Trickster made the thirteenth at table when he crashed a banquet of the gods, the consequence being the death of Balder the Good, god of light. Jesus plus twelve disciples made thirteen for an ill-omened seder on Maundy Thursday. As a consequence of the Crucifixion on the following day, Christians have long held Friday the thirteenth to be doubly unlucky.

Curiously, the thirteenth of the month is more likely to fall on a Friday than on any other day of the week, a fact whose proof was published in its essentials in 1969 in *The Mathematical Gazette* by a thirteen-year-old schoolboy at Eton named S. R. Baxter.

Why isn't each weekday equally likely? In any one year, the thirteenth occurs twelve times, once in each month. These twelve occurrences cannot be evenly distributed among seven weekdays. Similarly, the seven weekdays cannot equally share the forty-eight "thirteenths" occurring in any four-year period, which typically contains a leap year. However, our calendar uses neither a one-year nor a four-year cycle, but a four-hundred-year cycle; there are ninety-seven leap days every four hundred years, so arranged because a solar year is very nearly 365 plus 97/400 days. In four hundred years, forty-eight hundred "thirteenths" occur, and seven weekdays cannot evenly share them: 7 does not divide 4,800. In four hundred years, then, some weekdays will have more "thirteenths" than others. So the assumption that one cycle of our calendar evenly distributes the "thirteenths" among the various weekdays is false.

Furthermore, consecutive quadricentennial periods begin on the same weekday, because four hundred years contains an even number of weeks. Thus, every cycle of our calendar distributes the "thirteenths" identically; if one cycle unfairly burdens Friday, so will the next cycle and every subsequent one.

What remains is actually to count the distribution of "thirteenths" among the various weekdays for a typical four-hundred-year cycle, say from 1753–2152. And the winner is . . . Friday.

Sunday	Monday	Tuesday	Wednesday	Thursday	Friday	Saturday
687	685	685	687	684	688	684

Why start with 1753? Because the last major calendar reform occurred in 1752, dictating that an intercalary day be added to every year divisible by 4 except those years divisible by 100 and indivisible by 400. (For example, 1800, 1900, and 2100 are not leap years, because 100 divides them and 400 doesn't.) This is part of the fine-tuning of the calendar adopted by most of Europe thanks to Ugo Buoncompagni, better remembered today as Pope Gregory XIII, who promulgated the Gregorian Computation of the year in 1582. Protestant England ignored the innovation, which couldn't have come at a worse time in Anglo-Papal relations: On Gregory's death, in 1585, Felice Peretti became Pope Sixtus V and shortly thereafter issued what Elizabeth's counselor William Cecil, Lord Burghley, called a "roaring hellish bull" that excommunicated the queen and absolved her subjects of allegiance. Meanwhile, Philip of Spain was already assembling the Armada, with the pope's blessing if not financial backing. Britons had good reason to equate Catholicism with subversion, and few would have given a calendar reform from Rome the time of day.

As a result, England continued to use the Julian calendar until 1751, when Philip Dormer Stanhope, Lord Chesterfield, introduced a bill in Parliament to bring England's calendar in line with the Continent's, trimming eleven days from September 1752—September 3 through 13, to be precise.

This outraged an awful lot of people, such as those who found they had to pay a full quarter's rent for a little over two and a half months' stay; and "Give us back our eleven days!" became a popular rallying cry. (Some complained their lives had actually been cut short by eleven days.) Under the Chesterfield scheme, note that September 1752 had no thirteenth of the month at all. Had it not been deleted, the thirteenth would, in fact, have fallen on a Friday.

As it was, the thirteenth was allowed to fall through the cracks, contrary, as it happens, to the behavior of that number when confronted with one or another of the more common mathematical sieves, of which the most famous is probably the one invented by Eratosthenes to generate the prime numbers, which works like this:

Write down all the positive integers (or as many as you like), omitting 1 (which most Greeks didn't consider to be an integer):

Figure 46: The Positive Integers

2 3 4 5 6 7 8 9 10
11 12 13 14 15 16 17 18 19 20
21 22 23 24 25 26 27 28 29 30
31 32 33 34 35 36 37 ...

Cross out all integers of which 2 is an aliquot part (i.e., cross out everything that can be evenly divided by 2 except for 2 itself):

Figure 47: Eratosthenes's Sieve (First Shake)

2 3 4̸ 5 6̸ 7 8̸ 9 1̸0̸
11 1̸2̸ 13 1̸4̸ 15 1̸6̸ 17 1̸8̸ 19 2̸0̸
21 2̸2̸ 23 2̸4̸ 25 2̸6̸ 27 2̸8̸ 29 3̸0̸
31 3̸2̸ 33 3̸4̸ 35 3̸6̸ 37 ...

Cross out all integers of which 3 is an aliquot part (i.e., cross out everything that can be evenly divided by 3 except for 3 itself):

Figure 48: Eratosthenes's Sieve (Second Shake)

2 3 4̸ 5 6̸ 7 8̸ 9̸ 1̸0̸
11 1̸2̸ 13 1̸4̸ 1̸5̸ 1̸6̸ 17 1̸8̸ 19 2̸0̸
2̸1̸ 2̸2̸ 23 2̸4̸ 25 2̸6̸ 2̸7̸ 28 29 3̸0̸
31 3̸2̸ 3̸3̸ 3̸4̸ 35 3̸6̸ 37 ...

Cross out all integers of which 5 is an aliquot part . . .

Figure 49: Eratosthenes's Sieve (Third Shake)

$$2 \quad 3 \quad \cancel{4} \quad 5 \quad \cancel{6} \quad 7 \quad \cancel{8} \quad \cancel{9} \quad \cancel{10}$$

$$11 \quad \cancel{12} \quad 13 \quad \cancel{14} \quad \cancel{15} \quad \cancel{16} \quad 17 \quad \cancel{18} \quad 19 \quad \cancel{20}$$

$$\cancel{21} \quad \cancel{22} \quad 23 \quad \cancel{24} \quad \cancel{25} \quad \cancel{26} \quad \cancel{27} \quad \cancel{28} \quad 29 \quad \cancel{30}$$

$$31 \quad \cancel{32} \quad \cancel{33} \quad \cancel{34} \quad \cancel{35} \quad \cancel{36} \quad 37 \dots$$

and so on: Keep going on to the next number, skipping it, and crossing out all its multiples. You'll end up with a list of all primes between 1 and n^2, where n is the number whose multiples you are about to cross off. Thus, before you cross off multiples of 5, your list shows all primes between 1 and 25.

Eratosthenes actually has you cross off some numbers several times. Six, for example, gets crossed off first as a multiple of 2 and again as a multiple of 3. This may seem a little inefficient, but it has some advantages: First, it's easy to conceptualize as a kind of pacing-off with two-foot strides, then three-foot ones, and so on. Second, if you keep track of how many times you stepped on a particular number, you know how many prime factors a given number has and, if you use a different crosser-offer each time through, as we have, you know what those prime factors are:

Figure 50: Eratosthenes's Sieve (with Factors)

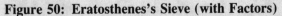

Eratosthenes's is not the only numerical sieve, nor indeed the only one that fails to winnow out the number 13: Consider the one described by the hydrogen bomb scientist Stanislaw Ulam and his colleagues at the Los Alamos Laboratories in 1956. Like Eratosthenes's, this one begins with the series of all positive integers (including 1), and entails counting out by increasingly larger intervals (or making your strides longer with each pass). The two sieves differ in the following respect, however: Where Eratosthenes has you stride through the same set of numbers several times, thereby crossing off some numbers more than once, Ulam dictates that during each pass, you stride through only those integers that have not been crossed out on any previous pass.

Starting at 1, cross out every second integer:

Figure 51: The Lucky Numbers (First Toss)

1 ~~2~~ 3 ~~4~~ 5 ~~6~~ 7 ~~8~~ 9 ~~10~~

11 ~~12~~ 13 ~~14~~ 15 ~~16~~ 17 ~~18~~ 19 ~~20~~

21 ~~22~~ 23 ~~24~~ 25 ~~26~~ 27 ~~28~~ 29 ~~30~~

31 ~~32~~ 33 ~~34~~ 35 ~~36~~ 37 ...

What's the second integer in the remaining series? 3. Starting at 1, cross out every third integer of those left.

Figure 52: The Lucky Numbers (Second Toss)

1	3	~~5~~	7	9
~~11~~	13	15	~~17~~	19
21	~~23~~	25	27	~~29~~
31	33	~~35~~	37 ...	

What's the third integer in the remaining series? 7. Starting at 1, cross out every seventh integer of those left.

Figure 53: The Lucky Numbers (Third Toss)

1	3		7	9
	13	15		~~19~~
21		25	27	
31	33		37 ...	

The fourth term in the remaining series is 9, so cross out every ninth term, and so on. Ulam called the numbers that slip through this sieve "lucky." He and his colleagues ran all positive integers up to 48,600 through this sieve and discovered that the number of lucky numbers was close to the number of primes in the same interval (and that the intervals between successive primes and between successive luckies grew at about the same proportion), that there were 715 numbers between 1 and 48,600 which were both luckies and primes, and that every even integer between 1 and 100,000 was the sum of two luckies.

In their article "On Certain Sequences of Integers Defined by Sieves," Ulam and his colleagues preface their findings concerning the lucky numbers by a description of two sieves: Eratosthenes's and another that they say "could perhaps be called a sieve of Flavius Josephus." The sieve of Flavius Josephus begins with all the positive integers (including 1) and a first step of eliminating every second integer, i.e., all the even numbers, and then strikes out every third integer from the sequence remaining. So far, the pattern is the same as with the lucky-number sieve. At this point, however, the Josephus sieve goes on to eliminate every fourth remaining number (leaving 1, 3, 7, 13, 15, 19, 25, 27, 31, 37, 39 . . .), then every fifth number (leaving 1, 3, 7, 13, 19, 25, 27, 31, 39 . . .), then every sixth, and so on.

"The learned Jew Josephus," as Coleridge's marginalia to the "Rime of the Ancient Mariner" calls him, was of priestly and royal descent. The Romans took him prisoner in Vespasian's campaign to suppress the rebellion in Palestine during the course of which the temple at Jerusalem was destroyed for the second time—a disaster commemorated ever since by pious Jews on the ninth of the month of Av as a holy day of mourning: Tishah-b'Av.

Josephus managed to ingratiate himself with Vespasian, by whom he was set free in A.D. 69 when the latter became emperor. Josephus wrote a number of books, including the *Antiquities of the Jews* and *History of the Jewish War*, in the latter of which he relates that shortly before his capture he was hiding in a cellar with about forty others determined not to fall into Roman hands alive. Rather than each dying by his own hand, they drew lots to be slain by each other, the man who drew the first to be killed by the man who drew the second, the second by the man who drew the third, and so on. As it turned out—"whether," Josephus says, "by chance, or by the providence of God"—he and another man were the last two left by the time the Romans arrived and took them into custody, whole and unharmed.

Josephus does not appear to have rigged the counting-out process by which the ordered lots were assigned to obtain his relatively high selective service number, though the wish to win such a seemingly random selection process by understanding and exploiting the algorithm that determines who gets to be "it" must be as old as counting out itself. For soldiers in the Roman army, the question was of decidedly more than academic interest: Every tenth man was ordered to be cut down in Roman legions that had mutinied, shown cowardice, or lost their eagle-topped standards in battle, as when the consul Appius Claudius's legion rebelled in 471 B.C. (The English term *decimate* is a pale reflection of this practice.) Variants of the counting-out problem are attested in Hegesippus's *De Bello Judaico*, written ca. A.D. 370, which states that Josephus saved himself by figuring the algorithm out. Several medieval works mention the problem, including Rabbi ben Ezra's *Ta'hbula,* to whom Elijah Levita attributed it when he published it in 1518; another early printed version appears in Buteo's *Logistica,* printed in 1559. Buteo begins the argument thus: "Fifteen Christians and an equal number of Jews are sailing on a boat that gets caught in a great storm . . ." Later it would become "Fifteen Christians and an equal number of Turks . . ." In any case, the idea is that to keep the ship from foundering, fifteen of the passengers have to be thrown overboard, and the problem is how to make sure that the good guys don't get selected to be thrown overboard when it comes time to do the counting out.

A Japanese version of this conundrum appeared in the *Mantoko Jinkō-ri* of Muramatsu Kudayu Mosei in 1665. One hundred thirty years later, Miyake Kenryu's *Shojutsu Sangaku Zuye* recast it as the story of a wicked stepmother's attempt to disinherit two stepchildren who are part of a ring of thirty kids circling a pond while she counts them out. (The stepmother is made to bungle the algorithm so that her own children lose out and the stepchildren inherit.) The underlying theme of all such problems is the appearance of fairness in yielding oneself up to chance or divine will, beneath which lies the puzzle solver's determination to stack the deck—by calculating the time sequence in reverse from where you want to end back to where you start. In other words, how do you work it so that you don't fall through the sieve into the water to your certain death?

Recall W. C. Fields's famous answer to the question, ''Is this a game of chance?''—''Not the way I play it.'' There are games of chance, and then there are games of skill. Most counting-out situations, like most card tricks, test the player's skill in solving problems of modular arithmetic—compare the ''clock face'' system where 8 o'clock plus 6 hours gets you to 2 o'clock (not 14).

In counting out, a player can predict who will be ''it'' if he knows: (1) the number of beats (stressed syllables) in the counting-out rhyme, (2) the number of players, (3) that person, within the circle of players, upon whom the chant will begin, and (4) a little bit about modular arithmetic. If there are five players, and the chant has seventeen beats, the clever player calculates that the first fifteen beats of the chant are superfluous, merely circling through the players three times before returning to the starting point. The final two beats are what count; the sixteenth beat brings the chant back to the starting point, and the seventeenth moves it to one person beyond. What's important is that 17/5 yields a remainder of 2—that is, 17 mod 5 = 2.

Using the same chant with seven players, the first fourteen beats are superfluous, merely effecting two laps through the circle of players. The fifteenth beat returns to the first player, and the sixteenth and seventeenth move two players beyond. The clever player does some quick modular math: 17 mod 7 yields 3; if I want to be counted out, I should position myself so the third beat of the chant occurs on me (that is, two players beyond where the chant begins). More elaborate calculations are required if there are to be multiple rounds of counting out (as in the story of the Christians and the Turks) and you *don't* want to get counted, but the principle is the same: It's all modular arithmetic.

Perhaps the best known of American children's counting-out algorithms is "Eeenie, Meanie, Miney Mo" (with seventeen or twenty-one beats, depending on the region), attested in the United States at least as far back as the Revolutionary War. That "catch a nigger by the toe" is racist was noted as early as 1850; accordingly, there have been a number of substitutions for "nigger," both the euphemistic (rabbit, black cat, baby, tiger) and the topically inimical if often no less racist (Indian, Hitler, Tojo, Viet Cong).

There are an astonishing number of variations on this rhyme, including "Eenty, teenty, tethery, methery . . . ," which has as its foundation an Old English country twenty-based counting system (possibly Welsh in origin) used by shepherds, fisherfolk, and knitters:

1. Yan	6. Sethera	11. Yan-dik	16. Yan-a-bumfit
2. Tan	7. Lethera	12. Tan-dik	17. Tan-a-bumfit
3. Tethera	8. Hovera	13. Tethera-dik	18. Tethera-bumfit
4. Methera	9. Dovera	14. Methera-dik	19. Methera-bumfit
5. Pimp	10. Dik	15. Bumfit	20. Jiggit

At "Jiggit" the counter takes a pebble from one pocket and puts it in another, and the count starts over.

LAZY EIGHT

To see a world in a grain of sand
And a heaven in a wild flower,
Hold infinity in the palm of your hand
And eternity in an hour.

—WILLIAM BLAKE

ALONG THE WAY to infinity, take time to appreciate some interesting numbers, of which there are infinitely many. In fact, no number is dull. Assume we could partition the numbers {1, 2, 3, . . .} into the interesting and the dull. Arranging the dull numbers in increasing order, we discover "the smallest dull number," an exceptional number indeed. For the set of dull numbers to exist, it must have a smallest—thus interesting—member. No number can be both interesting and uninteresting, so our assumption is false: The set of dull numbers is a null set.

"Interesting" is, of course, a mote in the eye of the beholder. C. P. Snow in his introduction to G. H. Hardy's autobiography, *A Mathematician's Apology*, tells of Hardy's visiting the number-theory genius Srinivasa Ramanujan, who was at that time ill and homebound. Hardy told Ramanujan that the taxi that had brought him there was #1729, and added that the number seemed uninteresting. Ramanujan immediately countered that 1,729 was a very interesting number indeed, being the smallest one that can be expressed as the sum of two cubes in two different ways, $10^3 + 9^3$ and $12^3 + 1^3$. The number 1,729 is also a Harshad number, i.e., a number divisible by the sum of its own digits (1,729 = 19 × 91, which has a nice symmetry to it besides).

''Randomness,'' too, is in the eye of the beholder. Asked to choose a random number between 10 and 20, more people choose 17 than any other number. Willfulness percolates: Subjects assess the randomness of the various choices and settle on 17, quite possibly because it is relatively prime with both 10 and 20. Subjects may also privately congratulate themselves about their selection, thinking full well that they've startled the researcher with their imagination and creativity. Cynical subjects might think they've foiled the researcher by choosing a number maximally unremarkable. Alas, so many people think this way, 17 becomes more remarkable than any other selection.

Seventeen: The title of a glossy magazine for the ''young adult'' market is the paradigm year of late adolescence, halfway between sixteen when one can try for a driver's license and eighteen when one can vote, get married in most states without parental by-your-leave, and, if one is a boy, get drafted into the armed forces. For many American seventeen-year-olds, high school graduation is not far off, and after that, what then?

Twenty: A *score,* the word itself from Scandinavian *skor* 'a notch (in a tally stick).' Notwithstanding our decimal culture, there's still a vestigial vigesimal element: Abraham Lincoln's gift for rhetoric shows itself in his most famous line, the beginning of the Gettysburg Address: ''Four score and seven years ago. . . .'' E. B. White says that with this felicitous substitution for a bald ''Eighty-seven years . . . ,'' Lincoln ''achieved cadence while skirting the edge of fanciness.''

It is a short leap from *score* in its original sense of '(make a) notch' to both the noun *score* as 'number of points earned by each side in a game' and the verb *score* as 'earn a point'; this last surely led to its metaphorical use in the 1950s among male adolescents as a euphemism for 'get to have intercourse.' In turn, for sixties counterculture survivors, *score* took on the additional meaning of 'buy some drugs.' *To know the score* has enjoyed long standing in standard American English, synonymous with 'to be on top of it/hip/nobody's fool,' or as the British used to say, 'to know what o'clock it is.'

A greater leap is to **Mersenne's number** (1,326,861,043,989, 720,531,776,085,755,060,905,614,293,539,359,890,333,525,802,

891,469,459,697): In the seventeenth century, Marin Mersenne said that he thought this number could be factored. It took a Cray supercomputer to prove Mersenne correct, two hundred years later. (It's equal to 178,230,287,214,063,289,511 × 61,676,882,198, 695,257,501,367 × 12,070,396,178,249,893,039,969,681.) When numbers get this big, how tempting to round them off to two significant digits and express them as powers of ten! For Mersenne's number one could simply use 1.3×10^{69}.

The googol: This is 1 with 100 zeros after it, or 10^{100}. The term is said to have been coined by the nine-year-old nephew of Edward Kasner, the mathematician who thought the number up; the two together then invented the *googolplex,* which is 10^{googol}.

Enormous numbers (like $10^{googolplex}$) have always fascinated people; but the boundary beyond which lies the truly *immense* (literally, 'immeasurable'), like the estimated size of the universe, has grown along with our collective ability to measure and quantify. George Bernard Shaw once remarked that for the Bushman eleven was myriad, being more than could be counted on one's fingers. For Mao Tse-tung, a hundred would do: "Let a hundred flowers bloom; let a hundred schools of thought contend," said the chairman at the height of the Great Proletarian Cultural Revolution (an ironic comment, considering the ruthlessly punitive orthodoxy that was the order of the day). In *The Play of Daniel,* which got its premiere at the Cathedral of Beauvais, France, sometime during the twelfth century A.D., a thousand was The Big Number: Of the attendants at Belshazzar's feast, it says *mille sonent modis,* 'Let them sing a thousand songs'—that is, 'Let them start singing, sing a whole lot of songs, and keep singing until they're told to stop.'

Nowadays we tend to talk of *millions.* A dollar ticket on the Tri-State Megabucks (joint lottery of the states of Maine, New Hampshire, and Vermont) has a shot at a pot that is about a million dollars, which is more money than most of us working stiffs know what to do with. If you stand on a street corner and give away a million dollars in ten-dollar bills at the rate of a ten-dollar bill a minute, it would take you a little better than two months to give the money away if you worked around the clock, and somewhat better than half a year if you worked more conventional hours (eight hours a day, five days a week).

Now, if you had a *billion* dollars to give away . . . Metaphorical spinoffs from the million and the billion abound, intensifying the sense of the uncountably large. We speak of a *bazillion* (probably a portmanteau word from *million/billion* and *bazooka*, the onomatopoeic name for the first shoulder-carried antitank rocket launchers of World War II). Ian Frazier in his story "The Killion" writes of a number so large that it kills you.

Even these numbers are finite—if you wrote them out, they would have a final digit. Not so with infinity, which by definition fails to terminate: *Terminus* was originally Latin for 'boundary stone,' as well as the name of the god charged with making sure such markers stayed put. The word *infinity* is ultimately from *fīnis* 'boundary, limit, end,' the same Latin root that gives English *final, finish, finite, definition,* and *fine*—both in its sense of 'neat-o, ne plus ultra,' and 'tops.'

A *finite verb* is one that can form the predicate of a sentence because it has a definite person, number, tense, and mood. *Fīnītus* was how Latin grammarians rendered the Greek term *horistikē*, from the verb *horizein* 'to divide, separate from, as a border or boundary; to limit; to determine.' The opposite of *fīnītus* is *infīnītus*—infinitive verb forms (e.g., "to be or not to be") are undefined in terms of who is doing whatever is going on with the verb and when. *Infīnītīvus* is the Latin rendering of Greek *aoristikē*, the past tense that, when students of Classical Greek first encounter it, whispers that the semantics of the Greek verb system may offer some tough conceptual sledding from here on in—indeed, that the verb system of Classical Greek is something of a tar pit. H. W. Smyth (the author of, for our money, the all-time best grammar book of Greek for speakers of English) says that the aorist "is so named because it does not show the limitation of continuance (expressed by the imperfect) or of completion with permanent result (expressed by the perfect)," a definitional boardinghouse reach of astounding skill and grace.

Ad infinitum is 'toward that which has no end or limit, i.e., infinity.' Greek and Roman mathematicians were so troubled by the infinite that instead of arguing that something went on ad infinitum, the Romans substituted the large-but-finite: "as large as you please" (*ad libitum*). The sign for infinity (∞)—which in fact only coincidentally resembles the cowboy brand dubbed *lazy eight*—was introduced by the British mathematician John Wallis in his 1655 treatise on conic sections. Wallis was a classical scholar, and it is possible that he derived ∞ from the old Roman sign for 1,000, CD, also written M—though it is also possible that he got the idea from the lowercase omega (ω), omega being the last letter of the Greek alphabet and thus a metaphor of long standing for the upper limit, the end.

The infinity shunned by the Greeks and Romans and vainly pursued by the natural number sequence is a border town, if you will, separating the land of natural numbers from the equally vast land of transfinite numbers, that is, numbers larger than any conceivable integer. Put another way, there are an infinite number of infinities, and the one you encounter at the outer reaches of the natural number sequence is merely the first, and in a real sense the smallest.

Let's turn up the heat on an earlier problem. Imagine a *really* big pile of bicycles; each bike is painted with an even number: 2, 4, 6, . . . all the way to infinity. Across the street teems a crowd. Each person has a hat; the hats are numbered 1, 2, 3, . . . up to infinity. One by one, folks mount bikes and hie to and fro, so the scene begins to look like Beijing on a shopping day. Are there enough bikes to go around?

Yes, because you can match up the bikes to the people, with no bike or pedestrian left over.

Figure 54: Bicycles and Riders (One on One)

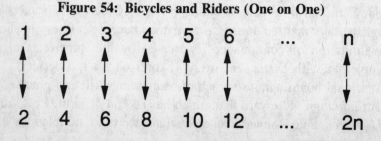

Comparing infinite sets differs little from comparing finite sets. In Chapter Six, we matched a finite set of bicycles and a finite set of cyclists the same way, without bothering to count individual members of either set. The sets were the same size because each bike had one rider and vice versa—no bikes or pedestrians left over.

Infinite sets challenge you to express a rule or formula that describes the one-to-one mapping universally, for any conceivable element from either set. Finite sets are less challenging, because they let you exhaustively list the matches. (E.g., Alex gets the blue bike, Joe gets the bike with the wicker basket, and Nick gets the other bike.) If you can find such a rule, the sets are the same size. If you cannot find such a rule, either you haven't looked hard enough or the sets really are different sizes.

Once you find a rule that looks good, you must prove it satisfies the condition that it matches each item from one set to exactly one item in the other, with no items left over. For the natural numbers and the even numbers, one such rule connects every natural number n with the even number $2n$, and the proof must show that:

- Every natural number connects to exactly one even positive number. (Or, in the correspondence between bicycles and cyclists, *every person has one bicycle*.)
- No two natural numbers connect to the same even positive number; if you pick two different natural numbers, they connect to two different even positive numbers. (*No bicycle is shared; if you pick two different people, they have two different bikes*.)
- Every even positive number connects to a natural number. (*Every bicycle gets used; none is left riderless*.)

Remember that we're dealing with sets here, and we want to arrange the sets side by side, like this:

Figure 55: Bicycles and Riders (Side by Side)

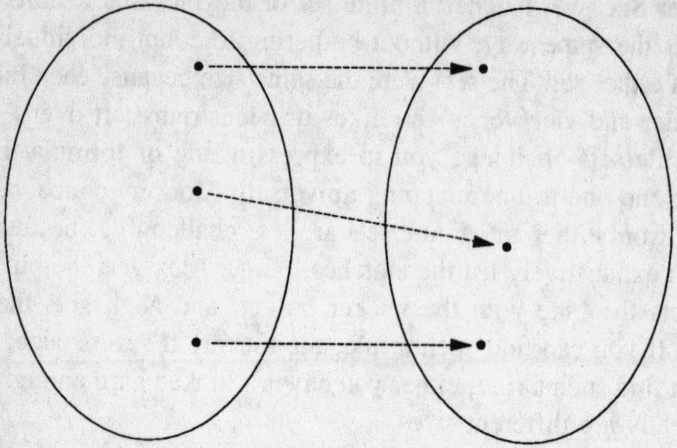

The proof simply ensures that the rule for arranging the sets side by side avoids the various pitfalls:

- A person with no bicycle (or a natural number with no corresponding even number)
- A person with two bicycles (or a natural number with two corresponding even numbers)
- An unridden bicycle (or an even number with no matching natural number)
- A shared bicycle (or an even number with two matching natural numbers)

Our rule avoids all the pitfalls, so the set of positive even numbers is just as big as the set of natural numbers. Strange, to be sure, because the set of natural numbers contains all the positive even numbers, plus a whole lot more. We're talking about infinity here, so things are allowed to get strange: An infinite set is any set from which you can remove some members without reducing its size. In fact, we can start with an infinite set, remove an infinite set, and still have an infinite set left behind, a magical feat we've already accomplished:

- Start with the natural numbers {1, 2, 3, . . .}
- Remove the positive odd numbers {1, 3, 5, . . .}
- Leave behind the positive evens {2, 4, 6, . . .}

The three sets are exactly the same size.

At this point, it might seem that infinity is an absolute upper limit, beyond which you can't go. But there are sets larger than the set of natural numbers. That is, you can find an infinite set with so many members that you cannot find a rule connecting its elements one for one with the elements of the natural numbers. One such set contains all real numbers between zero and one.

Georg Cantor first proved this by *reductio ad absurdum*. Assume, he said, that the sets are the same size. Then some function connects natural numbers to real numbers between zero and one, using up each number exactly once. That means we could (theoretically, given enough time) write a two-column list like this:

Natural Number	Real Number
1	.0123456 . . .
2	.4368276 . . .
3	.7689506 . . .
4	.5004000 . . .
5	.8544255 . . .
. . .	. . .

The list would stretch downward infinitely. Every natural number would be in the left column, and according to our assumption, every real number between zero and one would be in the right column.

Now for the logical absurdity disproving our assumption. There are numbers between zero and one not represented in the right column. Here's how to find one. First, circle the digits along the diagonal (upper left to lower right) of the right-hand column. That is, circle the "0" in the first number, the "3" in the second number, the "8" in the third number, and so on. Build a new number based on the digits you circled. Make sure that the first digit of the new number is not equal to the first digit you circled. Similarly, make sure the second digit is not equal to the second digit you circled, and so on.

Figure 56: Generating a New Real Number

$$.\textcircled{0}\,1\,2\,3\,4\,5\,6\,\ldots$$
$$.\,4\,\textcircled{3}\,6\,8\,2\,7\,6\,\ldots$$
$$.\,7\,6\,\textcircled{8}\,9\,5\,0\,6\,\ldots$$
$$.\,5\,0\,0\,\textcircled{4}\,0\,0\,0\,\ldots$$
$$.\,8\,5\,4\,4\,2\,5\,5\,\ldots$$

$$\ldots$$

For example, the first digit you circled is "0" (at the upper left corner of the diagonal). Therefore, make the first digit of your new number something other than 0, say 1. Number so far: .1

The second digit you circled is "3," so make the second digit something else, say 7. Number so far: .17

The third digit you circled is "8," so make the third digit something else, say 9. Number so far: .179

The fourth digit you circled is "4," so make the fourth digit something else, say 5. Number so far: .1785

As you continue this process, you gradually build a number that is between zero and one, but that does not appear in the right column. The number you are building differs from the first entry in the first digit, from the second entry in the second digit, and so on. There is our logical fallacy. Based on our assumption, the right column contains every number between zero and one. And yet, we can produce a number between zero and one that is not in the right column. Thus, our assumption—that the sets are the same size—must be false.

This proof is the beginning of modern set theory; it established that there are at least two sizes of infinity. One size of infinity is the size of the set of natural numbers. Sets that are the same size as the natural numbers are called *countable*, or *countably infinite*. Another, larger size of infinity is the size of the set of real numbers between zero and one; such a set is called *uncountable*.

To make matters worse, there are an infinite number of different sizes of infinity. Consider any set and the set of all its possible subsets. Are these sets the same size?

For the relatively simple case of non-null finite sets, the set of subsets is obviously larger than the original set. For example, for the two-element set {*a, b*} there are four possible subsets: { } (the null set), {*a*} only, {*b*} only, and the {*a,b*} pair. Is it also true for infinite sets? That is, is the set of subsets of any infinite set larger than the original infinite set?

Imagine two buckets, at your left and right feet, each containing a complete copy of the same infinite set. With your left hand, you can hold one element at a time, taken from the left bucket. With your right hand, you can scoop any number of elements from the identical bucket on your right. Your right hand, then, can hold any possible subset of the original set. Your left hand has infinite possibilities, because there are infinitely many individual elements it could snatch from the bucket. Your right hand also has infinite possibilities, because there are infinitely many subsets you can ladle up from the right bucket. The question: Is the right hand's infinite potential less than, equal to, or greater than the left's?

Assume that the two infinite sets are the same size. Thus, some mapping exists matching each subset with exactly one individual element of the original set. Each individual pairing (individual element in your left hand, subset in your right) can be classified with the following Yes-or-No question: Does the individual element in your left hand also appear somewhere in your right?

If the subset (in your right hand) includes its corresponding element (in your left), call the element *clannish;* if the subset excludes the element, call the element *unsociable*. Now consider the set of all unsociable elements. (That is, scoop all the unsociable elements from the right bucket into your right hand.) As a subset of the original set, this ought to match with some individual element you can hold in your left. (That's what our assumption about the two sets being the same size tells us, that each subset matches with an individual element.) What kind of individual element—clannish or unsociable—should you put in your left hand?

The individual (left-hand) element cannot be unsociable, because it would match an element in your right hand: Such matches define clannishness, making the left-hand element both clannish and unsociable, which makes no sense. But the left-hand element cannot be clannish, because by definition clannish elements appear in their corresponding subsets, and the corresponding subset (in your right hand) contains no clannish member whatsoever.

So there exists a particular subset—the set of all unsociable elements—whose corresponding individual element cannot exist, because it is neither clannish nor unsociable. Thus, the mapping from the set of individual elements (each held in turn in your left hand) to subsets (held in turn in your right) cannot be exhaustive; some subsets will be missed. The sets are not the same size, and the right hand's infinite potential exceeds the left's.

It matters not how large an infinite set the buckets at your feet contain. The set of all its subsets is larger. For *any* infinite set, a larger infinite set can always be found, leading to an infinitude of infinities.

Where will it all end?

INDEX